THE SCALE-UP LEADER

Your Guide to the Next Level of Success

Stuart Ross

Copyright © 2022 by Stuart Ross

All rights reserved. No part of this publication may be reproduced, stored in a retrieval system, or transmitted in any form, by any means, without expressed written consent.

Printed in the United Kingdom

Table of Contents

Chapter 1: How to Use This Book	1
Chapter 2: The High Growth Model	11
Chapter 3: Making the Decision to Grow	21
Chapter 4: Interested vs. Committed	41
Chapter 5: Enjoy the Journey	50
Chapter 6: Strategy One: Develop the Right Habits	63
Chapter 7: Strategy Two: First Who, Then What	85
Chapter 8: Strategy Three: Letting Go	97
Chapter 9: Strategy Four: Live in the Future, but be Present in the Now	106
Chapter 10: Strategy Five: Develop a Growth Mindset	118
Chapter 11: Strategy Six: Be a Clockbuilder	131
Chapter 12: Strategy Seven: Become a Multiplier	140
Chapter 13: Strategy Eight: Think Slow	150
Chapter 14: Strategy Nine: Be Unfuckwithable	162
Chapter 15: Strategy 10: Master your Tennis Game	176
Chapter 16: Closing Thoughts	194
What Makes High Growth Unique?	203
Bibliography	205
Index	211

CHAPTER 1

How to Use This Book

> *"The last 10% it takes to launch something takes as much energy as the first 90%."*
> **-Rob Kalin**

> *"If you are not embarrassed by the first version of your product, you've launched too late."*
> **-Reid Hoffman**

It's been a few years since my last book, and none of us could have possibly imagined the shocking events of recent times. The long-term ramifications of the pandemic are still unfolding before our eyes. What has remained constant is the need to be agile, to learn, to innovate, and to use all the tactics at our disposal to not only survive the pandemic, but thrive in the aftermath.

While new companies emerged during the pandemic, many of us took a pause, a moment for reflection and perhaps the chance to drill down into our business models and look at ways we could improve our mindsets, the way we conduct ourselves and our business. And that's what this book is all about - developing a scale up leader mindset to enable you not only to grow but thrive, no matter what the business environment throws at us.

I can very quickly teach you all the tools, methodologies and approaches to scale any business - but this is *not* what holds back most businesses.

What holds back most businesses is the **leaders**.

They need the mindset, belief, habits and tools to grow faster than their business, teams and competitors, for example. This book is about developing and honing the best leadership skills to help scale your business.

You might have been operating as a "lifestyle business" for some time now. If that's the case, congratulations are in order - but now, in a wave of post-pandemic positivity, you're looking to work towards becoming a scale-up business.

But what is a scale-up business? In short, it's scaling up your business to new heights. You've achieved an impressive level of growth, with an average annualised return of at least 20% in the past three years and with at least ten staff (according to the OECD definition).

You've possibly already received funding, and now you are entering into a period of high growth. But that might feel like a mountain…

Well, my task - and my passion - is to guide you up that 'mountain', walking alongside you, showing you shortcuts, helping you achieve the right mindset and beliefs, avoiding potholes, and making sure you stay focused, keeping energy and motivation high, as you embark on the journey to scale up your organisation or business.

Too many companies view scaling up as something beyond their control. They assume it's all down to luck. They have no idea that it is the result of disciplined management practices and adopting the right behaviours. It's not easy, but the chapters ahead of you lay it down in clear, simple steps, making it an interesting, fun journey to success.

This book aims to break down and explain these practices and behaviours, backed by a vital, overarching idea - to *enjoy* the journey.

Expect tips, tricks, and buckets of anecdotes. And in the long term, expect to gain skills for business and life that will serve you well.

Why This Book, Now?

Why the interest now? Well, we're coming out of COVID and there's an increased focus from governments not only in the UK, but also around the world, to really focus on scale-up organisations; those organisations really wanting to grow.

The challenge is that there are a lot of organisations which really haven't got the skills or the leadership to actually go and scale-up from where they are now.

I've had the good fortune to teach in the scale-up field for the last 15 years. But I *actually* spend comparatively little time teaching what companies should be doing.

What I *do* spend the bulk of my time on is working with leaders and leadership teams making sure they've got the right **mindset**, making sure they are committed, making sure they've got themselves in the right place in terms of beliefs, habits, values and identities.

These long-held beliefs, values and identities are often precisely what is holding them back - holding **you** back - to go scale the business and take people as individuals, as teams, and as a business, to places they've never been before.

That's the simple reason for this book.

We will identify 10 key leadership areas or skills, carefully chosen to ensure you approach your rapidly changing business with the right mindset, the right tools and a plan of action geared up for ongoing success.

We will give you a lot of practical advice and exercises to guide you on your journey to scale-up leadership excellence.

This book distils my scale-up leadership knowledge, gleaned by working with hundreds of organisation leaders. We've helped them embark on the scale-up journey and made sure - importantly - that they enjoy the journey, but also ensuring the journey is relatively effortless, compared to a 'trial and error' type route they may have gone down previously.

I hope this book enables you to better understand and embrace your own leadership journey with joy.

About Stuart Ross

After a successful senior corporate career, Stuart Ross followed his passion of helping both individuals and companies realise their potential and moved into personalised coaching and training with an emphasis on total improvement.

He founded High Growth in 2012 with a focus on scaling organisations. Initially focused in the UK's East Midlands, Stuart quickly developed an enviable international reputation with the results he helped companies achieve. His methodology and approach to scaling businesses quickly became adopted internationally including in Silicon Valley, Dubai, New Zealand and across Europe.

With publication of his top-selling books, _Growth Hacks_, _Needle Movers_, and _Secrets of High Growth Companies_, and the launch of the High Growth Academy, Stuart quickly gained further recognition across the UK and internationally.

A California office was created to complement High Growth's global presence and continue building out from the company's Nottingham, UK headquarters. Today, a network of accredited coaches delivers the High Growth methodology across the globe.

High Growth's Values

Integrity

We do what we say. We say what we mean. We accomplish our goals.

Commitment

We are 100% committed to our clients and to one another within the High Growth team. This ensures that we deliver results both to the organisations who hire us, and to the employees who deserve a better view.

Action

We believe in action. If we take action, we move forward either successfully or in the pursuit of knowledge that we can and will act upon.

Learning

We will only achieve long term success if we learn faster and more effectively than our competitors, but more importantly, we must implement these learnings deliberately and thoroughly.

Balance

We recognise our vision will grow as we grow. Therefore, our success is defined by where we are now. To enjoy our success now we must achieve a balance in all areas of our life.

How to Use this Book

I know what you're thinking "I can read, I know how to use a book!"

Well, I'm not here to patronise or annoy you, rather help you begin this exciting period of growth in your business with a chance to re-evaluate some key basic skills - like reading, listening and learning.

First up, get yourself comfortable. Turn off distractions. Move away from your inbox, your phone, the TV and the tablet.

Take the time to create a safe, easy space in your office or home to read this book, and allow yourself to slowly digest what I'm revealing. Yes, there are exercises, and plenty of food for thought, so come armed with a pencil, pen, paper, digital notepad - whatever it takes to help you note key points and lock them down in your memory.

It's a well-known fact that learning via listening or reading is bolstered by note-taking. In effect, you're taking the information in twice. And remember, in taking notes, you're freeing up your mind from the unenviable task of remembering everything.

Our parents certainly didn't teach us this, nor approve, but I'm offering you *carte blanche* to write in the margins. Highlight text, use a digital highlighter or stamp, scribble, however you like. This is your book and your journey. If you've downloaded it, why not print it off? This isn't a prescriptive textbook, it's a learning tool, and it's up to you how you ensure you get the most out of it - just like in business and in life.

The book is something of a distillation of all the lessons, ideas, hints and tips I've gleaned in my own professional experience of more than 20 years as a Founder, Director or coach of scaling companies.

I hope the insights you gain from these pages will help you achieve the growth you aspire to deliver in your company and in yourself. But it's a two-way journey. To benefit fully, you must take action. Take on board the ideas, the exercises, and by all means, talk to us for more information. Let me know what works for you, and what you find doesn't.

This isn't a book to simply read. Nor is it one to read in a linear fashion. You can dip in and out as your time allows; all I ask is that you don't simply read it, and simply add it to your (digital) bookshelf.

Always remember - for knowledge to stick, you have to start taking action immediately.

And each chapter includes exercise and action points, so you can immediately start your journey to becoming a scale-up leader and begin developing the right habits.

We start by ensuring you understand what we mean by 'scale-up' and help you are ready for the journey. Then, we share the 10 habits of scale-up leaders - based on 15 years of research - which are real game changers.

As you work through the book, think about how you might implement some of the core principles. Question the way you do things, and evaluate how you might do them in future.

For personal success, you face some hard decisions. I'm here to help give you insights into yourself and navigate the choppy waters of tough decision making.

Finally, by the time you've finished the book, I hope you'll be armed with a set of clearly defined new actions - to help you get where you want to be and be who you need to be.

For the next four weeks after reading the book, share your actions and goals wide and far, see how well you can implement them, then focus on implementing changes you've identified, every day.

Good luck on your journey - remember you've already taken a bold step in the right direction in getting a copy of this book. And as Goethe put it:

> *"Whatever you do, or dream you can, begin it. Boldness has genius and power and magic in it."*
> **-Johann Wolfgang von Goethe**

> *"All progress takes place outside the comfort zone."*
> **-Michael John Bobak**

> *"If you really look closely, most overnight successes took a long time."*
> **- Steve Jobs**

Exercise: Is Your Business Ready to Scale?

Before you turn another page, stop and think about the following - and note your answers:

1. **Do you have a compelling vision?**

Have you identified and articulated a purpose to resolve a large, urgent need through an ambitious, future-oriented, and innovative business concept?

2. **Is the market strong, and ready for your products and services?**

The market provides you with the tailwind – market size, growth and industry margins.

3. **Do you have enough loyal, delighted customers?**

Is your audience buying your product "just as fast as you can make it" because it is significantly better than any competitive product and fills an urgent need?

4. **What is your competitive edge?**

What makes your company, product and/or services distinctive? Something owned, mastery of skills, or a privileged relationship?

5. **Do you have a scalable model?**

Are you enjoying increasing returns, viral dynamics, improvement through use and economies of scale?

6. **Do you have the cash flow/access to funds to facilitate growth?**

Coaching Questions

Ask yourself the following questions and be sure to make a note of your answers:

What do you want to get out of this book?

What time will you create to study this book?

How will you ensure action is taken from the learning and insights you gain?

CHAPTER 2

The High Growth Model

> "First mover advantage doesn't go to the first company that launches; it goes to the first company that scales."
> **-Reid Hoffman, co-founder of LinkedIn**

> "Get five or six of your smartest friends in a room and ask them to rate your idea."
> **-Mark Pincus**

> "Dreaming, after all, is a form of planning."
> **-Gloria Steinem**

My entire business is based around scale-up companies – but what exactly do we mean by this?

As mentioned in the previous chapter, the Organisation for Economic Cooperation and Development (OECD) defines a scale-up company as 'any firm with a minimum of ten employees at the beginning of a three-year period that achieves an average annualised employment growth greater than 20 per cent over that period'.

Over my career and through my experience, I've embellished that definition. My description of a scale-up company is one that has *also* attained double-digit growth on its bottom line over the same time period.

For context, the latest available figures (2020) from the UK Scale Up Institute suggest private scale-up organisations have swelled to more than seven thousand, growing from 5,456 to 7,474 in a year – an increase of 37%.

At High Growth, we've worked with more than 2,500 companies to deliver and sustain fast growth. And we've found one big misconception that prevents most businesses from reaching new heights.

As we've already discussed, most companies see high growth as something **beyond their control,** possibly prompted by a sudden change in customer behaviour or a favourable bump in the economy.

This is the big misconception that I'm here to break.

What Will You Choose to Do?

The simple truth is, achieving high growth is a **choice**.

All it requires is discipline and a willingness to adopt the right management practices.

When you first start your business, it's all about proving you have a business model that works.

This can involve testing and tweaking areas like sales, marketing and operations until your company delivers a consistent return on investment.

Then there's a fork in the road where your company has an option to move into high growth - if you choose this route.

And there are four key skill areas that require development and focus if you choose the high growth path. It's these key skill areas that separate successful scale-up companies from the rest of the pack.

These are:

- Awesome leadership
- Developing a high growth team

- Creating a cutting-edge strategy, and
- Implementing your strategy faster and more effectively than competitors

Another simple truth: Unless these areas are continuously mastered, your company's potential will never be realised.

And always remember: "Today's excellent is tomorrow's good."

This book is here to help and provides some of the tools required to develop the scale-up leadership traits you'll need to adopt to succeed.

Following the tips and tricks laid out in these pages, you can achieve high growth, and stretch your entire business to its fullest potential, *predictably and sustainably*.

In my experience, scale-up companies have qualities and characteristics that go far beyond the numbers. Let's take a look:

Characteristics of a Successful Scale-Up Company

Casual observers might comment that a successful scaling company has simply been in the right place at the right time (note the rise of face mask distributors in the last year).

Others might suggest scaling companies have more time and resources than rivals; stronger leadership, a great team or simply good products and services. They might further add that scale-up companies have better-identified market opportunities, or have a well-defined strategy, which is then well-executed.

While all of these factors **do** play a role in modern business success, it remains the case that very few actually go on to achieve scale-up status.

In my experience, the heart of the problem is a failure to adopt the right management practices in a disciplined way. In other words, it's about adopting the right leadership mindset.

High growth is only possible if you learn and grow faster than the company does.

A scale-up company holds the ability to adapt and be flexible enough in the market to consistently stay ahead of the competition.

Exercise: Characteristics of a Successful Scale-Up Company

Scale-up companies also tend to share the following common characteristics. How many of the following can you tick off?

- ☐ A robust financial position
- ☐ A balanced combination of working capital and equity
- ☐ Arrangements in place for additional and contingency funds as required
- ☐ Achievement of above-average industry and sector profitability
- ☐ Multiple opportunities for/achievement of rapid revenue growth
- ☐ A strong brand identity, profile and image
- ☐ Investment in new product development and a portfolio of products at different stages of the product life cycle
- ☐ A loyal base of customers whose needs they fully understand
- ☐ A focus on building their brand
- ☐ A market-leading position
- ☐ Identification and targeting of expanding and/or niche market segments
- ☐ Substantial resources devoted to innovation, research and development activities
- ☐ Winning of awards and recognition as an outstanding company in one or more categories
- ☐ Competition on product differentiation, quality and/or service rather than price
- ☐ A high-performance management team with functional specialists and experts.

Do you fulfil the criteria?

Take a moment to consider the list of characteristics, and identify where you see any potential gaps or issues.

The High Growth Model

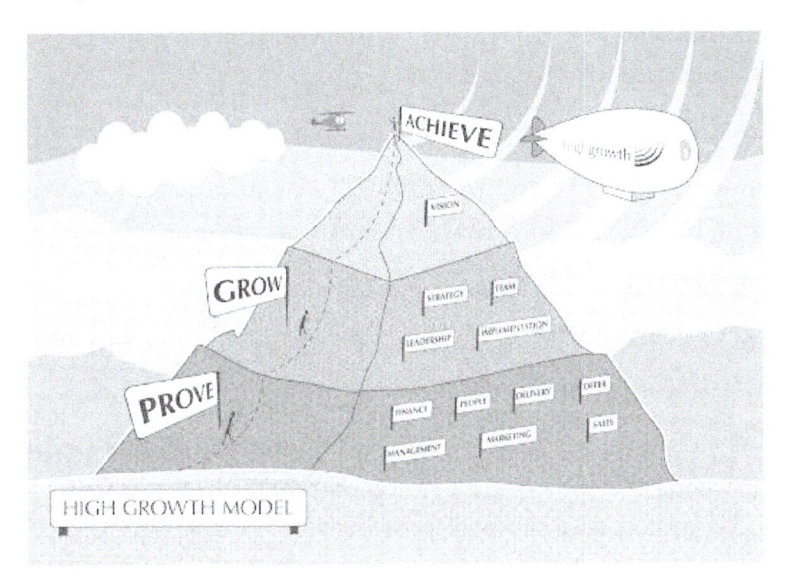

Of course, no company starts out as a high-growth business. There is a natural progression, or cycle, that every company must undertake before it achieves this enviable position.

Take a look at the descriptions below and reflect on where YOUR Company is at this moment in time.

The Prove Phase

When you start a business, your priority is to prove the business model is viable.

And at this time, company leaders often struggle to put the model in place, working long hours and involving themselves in every aspect of the business.

During the 'Prove Phase', most of us question ourselves constantly, asking: "Can the business deliver consistently, successfully, and make a profit?"

In the Prove Phase, your focus isn't just on putting processes in place, but on having a flexible team that can continue to refine the business model until the business works.

You'll be busy establishing systems for finance, human resources, management, marketing, sales and delivery, to name a few aspects, all in support of the company's goals.

But how do you know when you're ready to move out of the Prove Phase?

The simple test should pivot around whether or not you, the CEO, can step away from the business for a period of time and still have it run effectively.

If your business is at this stage, it has reached a crossroads.

For many companies, this is when the CEO steps back, satisfied that the business is making a good, steady income from a proven model.

Others decide to let the business remain at this stage indefinitely - happy to remain as a 'lifestyle business' Of course, standing still comes with risks. By failing to complete your business' growth cycle, it can get stuck in a rut, fail to keep up with the changing times or lose touch with customers. All can mean the end for your business.

In life, as in business, there are only two states - you are either growing or dying.

This is where the Growth Phase can make all the difference.

> *"To be the leader of a high growth company, you need to be energetic, disciplined, authentic, and have the right mindset."*
> **-Stuart Ross**

The Growth Phase

This phase is a choice. Some decide to stay at the lifestyle business model stage - for as long as it remains viable, with slow, steady growth. Others set their sights higher - and make the choice to embark on a scale-up journey.

A high growth company will reflect its leader's energy. The journey starts with the leader - it is the leader's commitment to growth that must energise and drive their companies. Such high growth company leaders have taken the bold, conscious choice to operate differently, to make life changes and to alter the way they do business.

High growth leaders embrace discipline and have demonstrated a willingness to adopt new skills and develop more refined thinking.

If you are serious in your desire to create a high growth company, you must commit to your continuing personal development as a leader.

Your Growth Phase needs the support and buy-in of a high-performance team, which must be led, motivated and inspired. Your leadership skills will also be challenged by the need to develop a plan to stay ahead of the competition and define a strategy.

The Growth Phase starts with leadership. It's down to you, as the leader, to define a compelling vision and be an example to the rest of the team in terms of behaviour and the way of being, for example, to drive the vision.

Develop your leadership skills, put faith and trust in your high-performance team, your strategy and consistent execution of that strategy, and then you can move into the final phase.

> *"As the leader of a company in its Growth Phase, you must be disciplined, measured, innovative, organised and efficient to stay ahead of the curve."*
> **-Stuart Ross**

The Achieve Phase

By now, with all your finely honed leadership skills, strategies and vision in place, you should be in a position to achieve/deliver your vision, with a commitment to personal growth and development of leadership skills, for example.

You are achieving what you set out to - but is it enough?

As a leader in the Achieve Phase, you face something of a dilemma: Do you stick with your current, successful company and re-define its vision before heading into another growth cycle, or do you move on, potentially starting a new business or pursuing another dream?

I can't, and probably shouldn't, make that decision for you. Only you can decide, but I hope you will know the right path to take when the time comes.

Coaching Questions:

Where is your business on the High Growth model?

What has prevented your business from moving to the next stage?

Why must you now move to the next stage of business growth?

What skills must you gain to start the scale-up journey?

Is your business ready to scale? What's holding it back?

CHAPTER 3

Making the Decision to Grow

"A hill is just another opportunity to leave your competition behind."
-Unknown

"No matter what, expect the unexpected. And whenever possible BE the unexpected."
- Lynda Barry

If you've established that you have the potential to become a scale-up - a proven business model delivering a consistent ROI, alongside all the other checks and balances I mentioned in the last chapter - then you're now *ready* to make the choice whether to scale. Congratulations!

You are considering if you are ready as an organisation to scale-up. You are satisfied you have a successful business model, a compelling vision, a great market and loyal customers. And let's not forget your bursting order book, and proof that you have enough cash - or, at the very least, reliable access to cash - to support scale-up growth.

These factors must be in place to embrace the scale-up journey - and give you the option to decide to embark on the scale-up journey. Now we must address you: you must make the decision.

You've decided the company is ready for growth. But - and here's the big question so many have missed - are YOU ready? And is this what you want?

You see, the scale-up leader must have certain characteristics, traits and habits in place to grasp the opportunity - and that's what this book is all about.

> *"There is at least one point in the history of any company when you have to change dramatically to rise to the next level of performance. Miss that moment, and you start to decline."*
> -- **Andy Grove, Intel CEO**

Murphy's Law, fixed

Back in my early corporate days, the office I worked in had a notice board. On that board, generally important information was communicated. One day a member of the team, as a joke, put a copy of Murphy's Law on it ("If anything can go wrong it will"). That depressing quote stared out at us as a team, until one day someone changed it to "If anything can go wrong, fix it!" Far more motivating!

> *"Let your joy be in your journey, not in some distant goal."*
> -**Apple CEO Tim Cook**

What Will You Choose?

Growth is a choice. I've said this a thousand times, and you know this. Yes, some companies are happy to stay at a certain level, relying on regular customers and happy to stay at the size they've grown to - i.e. a lifestyle business. But others are keen to keep growing.

As a company ready for scale-up, you have everything in place to continue your growth journey - at a good pace. But I appreciate - based on talking with hundreds of company leaders - that the decision to grow can be scary.

There is a fear of failure in us all. There is a responsibility to grow your company sustainably, and a responsibility to your staff, (who want to keep their jobs, and keep motivated), and to your wider stakeholders to ensure company success.

The journey of a scale-up should come with a health warning. It's not easy, nor should you expect it to be. It's certainly a personal journey of growth, during which your weaknesses, fears and vulnerabilities will be exposed.

You'll experience challenges, problems and difficult situations you may never have envisaged. Ultimately, you may well become someone very different to who you are today.

You could well be crippled by your own self-limiting beliefs.

The Identity Iceberg

```
The Results of
Our Efforts

        Being,
        Doing, Having

        Skills

        Beliefs

        Values

        Purpose

The
Determinants
of Our
Efforts/ Focus              Environment
```

The 'identity iceberg' theory visually describes a leader's ability to change. The tip of the iceberg represents your outward behaviour, your actions and decisions, and the resulting gains or losses.

As you know, only 10% of an iceberg is above the waterline; the rest remains hidden below. The same is true for people: we only see a small percentage of the characteristics that define someone. There are skills and beliefs that remain unknown in us all.

Above the waterline, see this section as your observable behaviours – your decisions and actions.

Below the waterline lie your skills, beliefs, values, and core identity.

> "The water that surrounds the iceberg is the environment in which you live and work."
> **-Brenda Hector**

Few people are aware that the decisions they make and the actions they take come from what's below. And what's below contributes to making you a successful leader.

Developing deeper self-awareness is key to understanding and exploring that 90% of what makes us *us*; the majority of our traits that lie below the waterline.

Exploring the bottom of the iceberg is tough. Changing our values and identity is difficult and challenging, but certainly not impossible.

When you're consistently not getting the results you desire, it's time to think about the iceberg that makes you who you are, and maybe begin chipping away at the mass of ice to create a new you.

Tony Robbins said the key difference between the life you're living now versus the life you were meant to live comes down to your own limiting beliefs. This applies just as much in business as personally.

Somewhere along the line, you may have subscribed to limiting professional beliefs.

Some examples of professional limiting beliefs might include:

"I could never build a multi-million turnover company."

"No one would invest that kind of money in my business."

"I'll never get the level of skills I need; I can't afford the best people in my industry."

"They would never want to partner with a company like us – especially at our size."

"Why would she take a meeting with me?"

"Reading and responding to email is a vital aspect of my business."

"We must be actively participating on every social media platform."

These are just a few examples I have heard in recent client coaching sessions.

The overarching fear in all of us is actually quite simple - the fear that "I am not enough". I've seen it so many times!

The key is to identify the most destructive limiting beliefs for you and your business and eradicate them.

How? One of the most effective ways I have come across is from Tony Robbins, called the "Dickens Process" a visualisation process that helps you really see clearly how your limiting beliefs have impacted your past, the present and, if you don't change, the future.

Getting rid of your limiting beliefs is not just about seeing how those have impacted your life up to now - and are likely to continue to influence your future decisions.

> *"It's not enough just to intellectually understand. You need to experience enough emotional pain to want to remove those limiting beliefs."*
> **-Bill Carmody**

A New Direction

For example, at a recent coaching session, we identified a particular person (a potential partner) a managing director needed to connect with. The MD's limiting belief was "*That person would never take a meeting with us.*"

This was reinforced by the people around him. Rather than focusing on all the reasons that person wouldn't have a meeting with him, we focused instead on the incredible value he can and will provide that person without asking for anything in return, or at the very least not upfront.

As the managing director thought about all of these things, he began to get excited and emotionally connected with the outcome, but then identified further barriers. For example, getting stopped by the potential partner's gatekeeper.

Through coaching we reframed this – the gatekeeper is simply there to stop the undetermined, unmotivated and unwilling from wasting that person's time.

So, our managing director must think differently. He can't do what everyone else has done and expect different results. It won't happen. Instead, he must be creative, innovative and someone who simply can't be ignored. He must make himself so valuable that the potential partner couldn't imagine *not* meeting. However, most importantly, he must take action.

The managing director did take decisive action, and through perseverance, gained a meeting with the potential partner.

The most important difference between *the successful* and *the hopeful* can easily be seen by the actions that have (or have not) been taken.

Many could, but the successful do – and that makes all the difference.

So, get rid of your limiting beliefs. If you don't think you can do this on your own (which, in itself is a limiting belief!) speak to a trained coach like me, who will help you.

> *"If you absolutely can't tolerate critics, then don't do anything new or interesting."*
> **-Jeff Bezos**

Get That Goal – But Keep Shooting For the Stars

Often, we believe it's all about achieving a goal, or a destination that will make us happy.

But nine times out of 10, when we hit that destination, we are still not happy.

This might be because we've moved on personally, or because things didn't turn out how we envisaged.

The key to remember here is that it's not about the destination, it's about enjoying the journey - and who you **become** along the way. You will have learnt lessons, perhaps acted differently, and grown as a result of the journey to the goal. But the short-lived satisfaction of achieving the goal should drive you on to define a new goal, and move forwards, armed with new knowledge and experience.

I said in a previous chapter how I'm here to help you climb the mountain.

Well, imagine at this point, having made the choice to embrace scaling-up, you are at the foot of the mountain, with all the correct equipment, food, maps and support in place. You are feeling fit, prepared and ready.

But you still need to double-check everything before you take that first, possibly scary, step up the rockface, right?

I can help you check your equipment, readiness and fitness, but only you can ultimately make the bold decision to take the first step up the mountain. Make the decision proactively - and consciously - and don't feel pushed into it.

It's vitally important here to spend enough time making your decision, reflecting on it slowly.

A Desert Tale

There was a man who had developed the capacity to achieve whatever he put his mind to, whether material or spiritual aspirations. When asked who had guided him to such a high level of personal mastery, he replied that a dog had. On further questioning, he recounted the following tale.

"While travelling through the desert I came across a water hole where there was a dog almost dying of thirst standing by the water's edge."

"Each time the dog approached the water it saw its reflection and, assuming this was another dog protecting its territory, it became frightened and withdrew."

"I watched it moving toward the water and withdrawing until eventually, out of necessity, it cast away its fear and leapt into the water; at which moment, the 'other dog' vanished."

"Just as the dog discovered that the obstacle to what it sought was itself, I also realized the barriers to my own progress were created by my own thinking."

"This insight combined with courage and discipline has given me the freedom to 'jump in' and do what needs to be done."

Next, there are many tools that will help you re-evaluate your life; help you discover where you are and whether you are wholly committed to the scale-up journey. The tools are here - below - to help you make the decision whether to embark on the scale-up journey.

Why Do You Want to Scale-Up?

> *"There is nothing so useless as doing efficiently that which should not have been done at all."*
> **-Peter Drucker**

Here are the questions and exercises that will help you discover your motives for scaling your business.

How Balanced is Your Life?

You may be familiar with the wheel of life - a chance to examine how different aspects of your life mesh together.

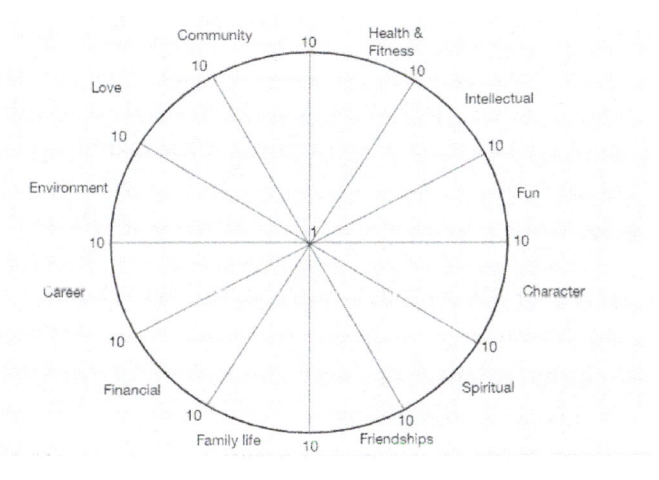

There are 12 areas of the Wheel of Life. Each area must be in balance with all the others and this is something we must all constantly work on.

The 12 areas are:

Health and fitness

- It goes without saying that your physical wellbeing must come first

- How do you want your health to be given your age and physical conditions?

Intellectual
- How much/how fast are you learning and growing?
- Everything you are and where you find yourself today is thanks to your thoughts and beliefs. Your mind creates your reality, which is why your intellectual life is of such importance.
- With an extraordinary mind, one that learns and adapts and works for you (not against you), you're unstoppable.

Fun
- We must allow time to experience the world and exciting things.
- When your time comes to leave this world behind, you want to go out like Frank Sinatra. You want to do it "your way".
- Who doesn't want to reflect back on their lives and feel good about the time they had?
- And in the end, as Abraham Lincoln put it: "it's not the years in your life that count. It's the life in your years."

Character
- What is your true character? Are there any parts of you that you're suppressing or are afraid to step into? Are you afraid to shine your light too brightly, or that you may be rejected if you were to step into your authentic self?
- Think about all the character traits that make up who you are, and who you'd love to be. Mary Ann Evans, known by her pen name George Eliot, said it best when she wrote: "It is never too late to be what you might have been."

Spiritual
- Your own sense of spirituality is what gives life meaning and depth. Reflecting on your relationship to the essence of life is the

foundation for a fulfilling existence, and without it, fear may take over.
- If you're new to spirituality and don't have any prior beliefs, don't fret. Put the feelers out and explore which ideologies work for you. Perhaps you could begin with some meditation, yoga and light reading about spirituality.

Friendships

- This is the support network you have.
- When you boil it down, we human beings are social animals. It goes without saying that it's near-on impossible to live a truly fulfilling life without a support network.

Love

- This area includes all your relationships, romantic and family.
- How happy are you in your relationships?

Career

- Think about how you are growing, progressing and excelling in your career.
- Do you feel stuck in a rut? Is your business thriving or stagnating?

Financial

- Having your finances in order is one of the first steps any of us would need to take to restore balance to the chaos that is modern life. After all, we live in a world where gaining and spending money is a necessity. Strike the balance between spending and saving.

Family Life

- Think about how successful your relationships with your partner, parents and siblings are.

- If you don't have immediate family, how is your relationship with your alternate family (like closest friends, or your 'extended' family)?

Environment
- How do you feel about the quality of your home, your office and the spaces where you spend your time?
- Could your environment be better? How comfortable do you feel in different spaces?

Community Life
- To what extent do you give back?
- Are you involved with your local community?
- Are you giving, contributing and playing a definite role in your community?

Put too much emphasis on one of the aspects of life identified in the wheel, above, and the other areas will suffer.

If you decide to fully commit to high growth, but have an existing health issue, for example, your health will simply start to deteriorate more, because you're focusing too much on the business - and that's counterproductive!

Thinking about the wheel and your own life, it helps identify how important your business is relative to other areas of your life. Business is but one part - you need to view it holistically - and consider where you are, relative to your vision in each segment.

If there's weakness in one segment, then this will only increase more if you solely focus on your business.

You are making trade-offs.

Ideally, we all want a smooth, balanced wheel, with all areas aligned, before you embark on your journey.

Life is not purely about business. It's about understanding, then taking, a holistic approach to every area of your life - that is what success is.

While your physical and mental wellbeing are crucial, they must remain in harmony with all other aspects of the wheel.

I believe a key factor is looking at work/life balance and ensuring you *enjoy* your business. Are your human needs being satisfied? What role does business play in your life, and how are your relationships outside of your work life?

I've spoken to enough C-level executives to understand that most successful people maintain a good balance in life.

Exercise: Map Out Your Wheel of Life

Decide where you are on the wheel - from 1 (very dissatisfied with that area) to 10 (very satisfied) for each area.

Map out your scores on the wheel, here, as an easy way to see where your life needs most work.

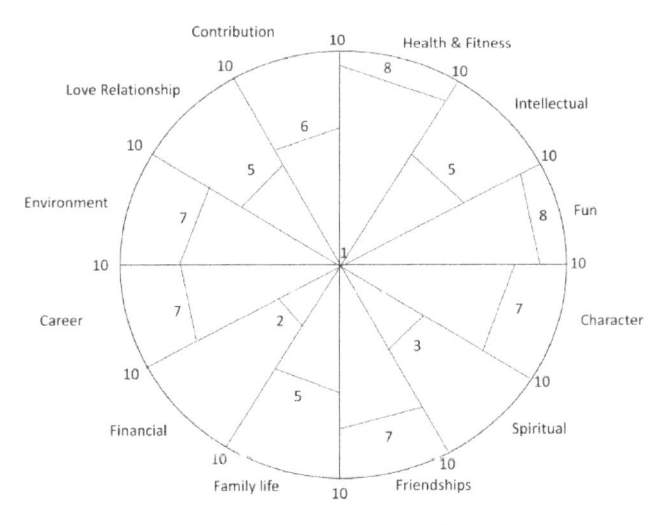

(See Emma-Louise, The Complete Guide to The Wheel of Life)

The original concept of The Wheel of Life is attributed to the late Paul J. Meyer who founded the Success Motivation® Institute in 1960. Paul J. Meyer was a thought leader and coaching industry pioneer. He built many programs to help people achieve their goals, manage time and be better leaders.

Entrepreneur Meyer launched and acquired more than 40 companies in a wide range of areas. These include motor racing, commercial and residential real estate, finance, printing and equipment leasing - and many more. More than half of these businesses failed, but he loved a challenge and believed, "Attitude is everything!"

What is Your Life Stage?

It's worth taking time out to examine what life stage you are at - which often depends on your age - and how your work fits in with other aspects of your life, such as your family and your own needs. Too many people concentrate entirely on work at all stages of life.

At different life stages, you will have a different focus. When we are young, work often dominates. As we grow older and maybe have children, a focus on family becomes more important…and all these shifts in balance are to be expected, depending on our life stage.

It's important, therefore, to be mindful of what life stage you are at, and what your focus needs to be over the next few years.

Burnout - especially with the pandemic - is too common. I've seen a lot of people who simply thought they could work their way through, and out of, the economic meltdown caused by coronavirus - but this simply isn't viable.

WHAT STAGE ARE YOU AT IN YOUR LIFE?

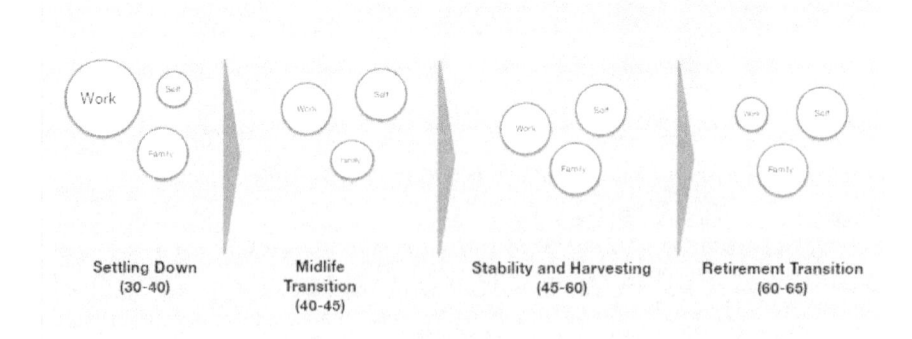

Settling Down (30-40)	Midlife Transition (40-45)	Stability and Harvesting (45-60)	Retirement Transition (60-65)

Ask which areas of your life need the most work before you commit to a high growth strategy. Aligning work, family and your self needs is key to success.

So, when you're 'settling down', between the ages of 30 to 40, your focus may be more on work.

As you perhaps start having kids and move more into midlife, you're focusing more on balancing self, family and work. And as we head towards retirement age, the focus then tends to be more on the self and the family, with reduced emphasis on work. As you get older, you want to pull back on work to enable you to spend more time in other areas.

Therefore, the later in life we find ourselves, the less risk-averse we naturally are, and our priorities naturally change.

Take a moment to think about what stage of life you are at, then:

Exercise: What Will Be Your Legacy?

Without getting too maudlin, imagine attending your own funeral.

What do you think people would say?

Take some time to think about the high and low points of your life - and what lessons you can take from those moments.

How would your best friend describe you and your life?

_____

_____

_____

_____

How would a professional colleague describe you and your life?

_____

_____

_____

_____

How would your family describe your life?

_____

_____

_____

_____

What would your local community say about you?

_____

_____

_____

> *"And in the end, it's not the years in your life that count; it's the life in your years."*
> **-Abraham Lincoln**

The Businessman and the Fisherman

One day a fisherman was lying on a beach, with his fishing pole propped up in the sand and a solitary fishing line cast out into the sparkling blue surf.

He was enjoying the warmth of the afternoon sun and the prospect of catching a fish.

About that time, a businessman came walking down the beach, trying to relieve some workday stress.

He noticed the fisherman sitting on the beach and decided to find out why this fisherman was fishing instead of working harder to make a living for himself and his family.

"You aren't going to catch many fish that way," said the businessman to the fisherman.

"You should be working rather than lying on the beach!"

The fisherman replied, "And what will my reward be?"

"Well, you can get bigger nets and catch more fish!" came the businessman's answer. "And then what will my reward be?" asked the fisherman, smiling.

The businessman replied, "You will make money and you'll be able to buy a boat, which will then result in larger catches of fish!"

"And then what will my reward be?" asked the fisherman again.

The businessman was beginning to get a little irritated with the fisherman's questions.

"You can buy a bigger boat, and hire some people to work for you!" he said.

"And then what will my reward be?" repeated the fisherman.

By now, the businessman was getting angry.

"Don't you understand? You can build up a fleet of fishing boats, sail all over the world, and let all your employees catch fish for you!"

Once again, the fisherman asked, "And then what will my reward be?"

The businessman was red with rage and shouted at the fisherman, "Don't you understand that you can become so rich that you will never have to work for your living again! You can spend all the rest of your days sitting on this beach, fishing, and admiring the scenery. You won't have a care in the world!"

The fisherman, still smiling, looked up and said, "And what do you think I'm doing right now?"

An adaptation of an original short story "Anekdote zur Senkung der Arbeitsmoral" ("Anecdote concerning the Lowering of Productivity"), published by Heinrich Böll, in 1963.

*See also Plutarch's Parallel Lives, and Simone de Beauvoir's first philosophical essay, Pyrrhus and Cineas

Coaching Questions:

Why do you want to scale your business?

_____
_____
_____
_____

Are all other areas of your life in balance to help make the scale-up journey easier?

_____
_____
_____
_____

What beliefs are holding you back from scaling your business successfully?

_____
_____
_____
_____

What is the purpose of your life? Does scaling a business align with this purpose?

_____
_____
_____

What skills do you have/need to develop to ensure a successful scale-up journey?

Are you at a stage of your life where you have the energy, time and motivation to embark on a scale-up journey?

What do you want your legacy to be?

What is your relationship like with the person in the mirror?

CHAPTER 4

Interested vs. Committed

> *"If you define yourself by how you differ from the competition, you're probably in trouble."*
> **-Omar Hamoui**

> *"There's a difference between interest and commitment. When you're interested in something, you do it only when it's convenient. When you're committed to something, you accept no excuses, only results."*
> **-Ken Blanchard**

Are you interested, or committed? There's a difference!

As the Ken Blanchard quote above explains, interest in something infers a hobby, a sport or a low-level passion. True commitment infers a true passion; an unwillingness to alter your path, and a focus on achieving what you set out to achieve.

Perhaps the best way to illustrate this point is with an anecdote. This one involves Philippe Petit, the daredevil trapeze artist who famously walked on a tightrope strung between New York's Twin Towers one misty morning in 1974.

Speaking afterwards in an interview, he said the most terrifying moment wasn't the first step; it was the second.

Upon taking the first step, you still have one foot on the building. You are relatively safe, you can turn back, and you still have one foot anchored and supported on something.

But with the second step, you have to shift your whole centre of gravity so the entire body is no longer supported by anything solid. In other words, you are 100% committed.

Our hero Philippe not only walked between the Twin Towers once but completed his death-defying aerial stunt repeatedly.

While I'm not asking you to do anything as dangerous as tightrope walking, taking the leap into scale-up leadership can leave you feeling as nervous as taking that second step onto the wire. Petit would never have stepped out if he hadn't checked the rigging the night before, had a trusted team and had complete faith in his own abilities and actions - despite unexpected wet weather.

All of this translates perfectly to you and your business. While we don't all have Petit's blind faith in our ability, the lesson is clear and simple: if we don't take that bold leap, we'll stay where we are.

Many people I've worked with and coached are merely interested in achieving goals or a vision.

They will generally come with excuses as to why they don't achieve that success, and they rarely go and achieve it. Again, this marks the difference between interest and commitment.

You demonstrate your commitment by your actions. Take your commitment to individuals, take your commitment to the team, and help grow their commitment to the vision of what you're trying to achieve as a business by your actions.

Your business and your team are a mirror of you. If you demonstrate your commitment in what you do, how you act and who you are on a daily basis - your team will mirror your commitment.

If you are 100% committed and you do what it takes, no matter what - you will go and take that bold second step. That level of commitment, faith in your chosen course of action and surety is what's really going to drive you forward.

Are you 100% committed to growth?

> *"Les limites existent seulement dans l'esprit de ceux qui ne savent pas rêver." (The limits exist only in the minds of those who can not dream)"*
> **-Philippe Petit**

Never start your scale-up journey unless you are 100% truly committed. If you're not, you're destined to fail, maybe not immediately, but in time - and your goals, or vision, will not be achieved. Perhaps failure is too strong a word, but you will most certainly face challenges and discover vulnerabilities, and it will undoubtedly be tough. If you're not 100% committed, you won't have the grit and determination to push through to get to your goals.

With the right level of focus, you can achieve your goals. You cannot be swayed in your vision; you cannot veer off into other ventures.

Check Your ID

Hitting the path to true commitment involves some soul searching, and for many of us, involves a realignment of who we even are. It's within your power to mould yourself into who you really want - or perhaps need - to be. You must be the person you need to be, as if your vision is delivered now. If you've ever heard Elon Musk talk about his vision for SpaceX, he talks as if it is upon us now, and he's working avidly and doggedly towards that ultimate goal - to make humanity a multi-planetary species. He's living that vision every day.

Exercise: What's Driving You?

Find your passion - what is your passion? Write down your main passions in life, and how much time and energy you spend on each of them.

Take your first steps. How scary is pursuing your goals? Write down your fears, and work through how to overcome them.

Have faith. How confident are you in your aims? How confident are you in the business?

Now's the time to examine any doubts - write them down - and again, take steps to assuage those doubts. Commitment will only come from a position of strength, knowledge and faith in your idea, yourself and your team.

Adapt to "a new you", and you set different standards for yourself. Everything you have right now is simply down to the standards you've set and accepted for yourself.

The path to commitment may involve a major step - a commitment to a new you. Change yourself, and you change the possible results and outcomes of your life. You'll start doing things differently and even look at your life through a refreshed perspective. Are you ready to make such a massive change?

The reality is that undertaking that commitment is not a smooth journey, nor is it easy. You will experience Satori and Kenshō moments on the journey - and these will be the moments of growth.

Satori and Kenshō

Have you had your satori moment? In Zen Buddhism, satori refers to a deep, abiding insight in which someone sees and understands the true nature of the universe and of reality itself. A moment of enlightenment.

In more practical, understandable terms, you could say a 'satori moment' is one of those rare moments in life when we realise our purpose or connect to what is really driving us. We need to seek out such moments, as they help us on our critical path to success.

> *"Satori moments are critical experiences. They are rare — maybe once a decade, or even once a lifetime. But when you have one, they will change your life. When they happen, you will know. They will change your life forever."*
> **-Dave Inder Comar**

Kenshō, meanwhile, refers to that initial moment of enlightenment. Enlightenment lite, if you like. Satori is a deep sense of fulfilled enlightenment; Kenshō is the inkling.

Perhaps Kenshō could be the idea of a business, the start up phase. Satori is what we move towards as we get deeper into our reasons for pursuing scale-up strategies.

Furthermore, Satori moments are seen as growth through sudden insights; those rare, unicorn moments. But Kenshō moments describe growth through pain - all too common in modern business!

Classic Kenshō moments are those where pain enters our lives but forces a (positive) shift. Examples might include starting a business, running out of cash or failure of a team member. They are painful experiences, right? But as an open-minded leader, you dust yourself down, examine what might have gone wrong, what went well and carry those lessons into your next venture.

You may be unfaltering in your ambition, but stress takes its toll and you fall ill. That's another painful experience - physically and mentally. But once you recover, you would surely make a commitment to take better care of your health.

These gradual, slow moments of growth are almost imperceptible to us, sometimes. But they are cumulative, building up over time to make us better, more adaptable, people who have learnt from our mistakes, and have *learnt to learn* from painful experiences.

Conversely, a Satori moment is pleasurable. A sudden revelation. A moment of clarity that might come from your life coach, a seminar, an article or blog, or a life-changing experience.

Sadly, we know Satori moments happen infrequently. But by immersing yourself in personal growth activities and experiences, you put yourself in the best position to receive inspiration. And remember, it's not only committing to personal growth, you must learn faster than the team who look to you for inspiration.

And inspiration is just what great leaders sometimes need.

Keep yourself open to, and aware of, these Kenshō and Satori moments and your growth journey will be easier and more interesting. Expect new ideas, insights and awakenings as you open yourself to these concepts and new ways of thinking.

Exercise: How Committed are You?

If you are committed, you'll typically demonstrate it with the following traits. Tick which applies to you.

- ☐ Make yourself go "all in" - even if you don't yet quite know how to achieve your goal(s). When you're "all in", nothing will stand in your way.
- ☐ Take bold, decisive actions, calling upon all your resourcefulness
- ☐ Hold beliefs, thoughts and ideas that are aligned with the success of the goal.
- ☐ Release yourself from needing approval and validation from others.
- ☐ Invest fully in achieving the goal (like hiring a coach, expert or other support personnel.)
- ☐ Swiftly address bottlenecks and roadblocks. A situation in the way of your success can steal your time and/or energy. As a committed business leader, you need to resolve any issues so you can get back to focusing on business.
- ☐ Show willingness to put yourself in uncomfortable situations and take action to achieve your aims
- ☐ A refusal to allow any excuses to overshadow your commitment.

Coaching Questions

Are you committed or interested in embarking on the scale-up journey?

Why must you embark on the scale-up journey now?

What does your first step on the journey look like?

How much would you say you enjoy the destinations compared with the journey?

How could you increase the meaning of successfully scaling your company without drastic change?

CHAPTER 5

Enjoy the Journey

> *"Life gives you plenty of time to do whatever you want to do if you stay in the present moment."*
> **-Deepak Chopra**

> *"Becoming isn't about arriving somewhere or achieving a certain aim. I see it instead as forward motion, a means of evolving, a way to reach continuously toward a better self. The journey doesn't end."*
> **-Michelle Obama**

I've mentioned this a few times already, but it's a key point in achieving success as the leader of a scale up company: **enjoy the journey**!

Sounds simple, right?

Fundamentally, it really is, but it's worth examining in more detail so you can define what you do and do not enjoy, and work from that basis to craft a life - both in business and personal terms - that is what you want it to be.

In reading this book, you've already declared - to some extent - that you are a person that loves business, loves a challenge and isn't afraid of growth. All admirable traits, but we must also remember that life has many facets that we strive to balance. It is only with this balance you can achieve true success.

If we live life out of balance in one or more areas, this ultimately impacts other areas of our life. For example, I have coached seemingly successful business people many times, who have neglected areas such as family or health. This has always ultimately led them to question whether the effort, time and resources invested in the business from a personal perspective was worth it.

If we are out of balance in life, it's easy to focus too much on one area than another - like our business over our health.

Part of enjoying the journey to a successful scale-up company is to decide how fast you want to grow.

And - you've guessed it already, I suspect - it's entirely your choice as to how fast you grow.

Your growth journey is exactly that - yours. The point to note here is that you can control and decide your company's growth rate, rather than having it imposed on you by others, or by external influences such as the market you compete in, or others' expectations.

The growth rate you aspire or commit to must lead to more focus, more/time and more effort from you spent on the business. And this will inevitably have an effect on other areas of your life - such as your relationships and health.

Are you willing to make that trade-off?

Or is it better to find a pace that allows you to keep a good balance in all areas of your life? Remember the higher the target business growth, the more time and commitment will be required from you as a leader.

It's about building your business around your life, not your life around your business. Make sure the business serves you, not the other way around!

Enjoy the Journey

The Station, by Robert J Hastings

Tucked away in our subconscious minds is an idyllic vision.

We see ourselves on a long, long trip that almost spans a continent.

We're travelling by passenger train, and – out the windows – we drink in the passing scene of cars on nearby highways, of children waving at a crossing, of cattle grazing on a distant hillside, of smoke pouring from a power plant, of row upon row of corn and wheat, of flatlands and valleys, of mountains and rolling hills, of biting winter and blazing summer and cavorting spring and docile fall.

But uppermost in our minds is the final destination. On a certain day, at a certain hour, we will pull into the station.

There will be bands playing and flags waving. And once we get there, so many wonderful dreams will come to us. So many wishes will be fulfilled and so many pieces of our lives will be neatly fitted together like a completed jigsaw puzzle. How restlessly we pace the aisles, damning the minutes for loitering.... Waiting, waiting, waiting, for the station.

However, sooner or later we must realise there is no one at the station, no one place to arrive at once and for all. The true joy of life is the trip. The station is only a dream. It constantly outdistances us.

"When we reach the station, that will be it!" we cry. Translated it means. "When I'm 18, that will be it! When I buy a new 450 SL Mercedes Benz, that will be it! When I put the last kid through college, that will be it! When we have paid off the mortgage, that will be it! When I win a promotion, that will be it! When I reach the age of retirement, that will be it! I shall live happily ever after!"

Unfortunately, once we get it, then it disappears. The station somehow hides at the end of an endless track.

"Relish the moment" is a good motto, especially when coupled with Psalm 118:24 *"This is the day which the Lord hath made; we will rejoice and be glad in it."*

It isn't the burdens of today that drive men mad. Rather, it is regret over yesterday or fear of tomorrow. Regret and fear are twin thieves who would rob us of today.

So, stop pacing the aisles and counting the miles. Instead, climb more mountains, eat more ice cream, go barefoot more often, swim more rivers, watch more sunsets, laugh more and cry less.

Life must be lived as we go along.

The station will come soon enough.

The Station story hits the nail on the head. We must ensure our life and business goals are aligned, and be sure to enjoy the journey.

Back in the early 2000s, business authors Jim Collins and Morten T. Hansen, along with a team of 20 researchers, set out to answer: "Why do some companies thrive in uncertainty, even chaos, and others do not?"

After NINE years of research, the results became a bestselling book, Great by Choice. In the book, Collins and Hansen reveal that some of our most renowned, well-known and well-loved corporations are where they are today for a simple reason - they stuck to the plan!

Obviously, there's a little more to it than that (*I recommend checking the book out*), but in short, major companies that have achieved long-term success seem to have something in common - they had a clearly defined growth strategy, and carefully, methodically, and consistently stuck with that plan. Eyeing long-term goals, they enjoyed the journey. They are not companies that get side-tracked by change, by fear or by unpredictable, ever-changing circumstances.

The rare companies whittled down in Collins' and Hansen's research were dubbed the '10Xers' - because they beat their industry index by at least 10 times. In other words, steady, controlled, disciplined growth saw them achieve *ten times* the success of their competitors!

> "Yet some companies and leaders navigate this [disordered] world exceptionally well. They don't merely react; they create. They don't merely survive; they prevail. They don't merely succeed; they thrive. They build great enterprises that can endure. We do not believe that chaos,

> *uncertainty, and instability are good; companies, leaders, organizations, and societies do not thrive on chaos. But they can thrive in chaos."*
> **-Jim Collins, Great By Choice**

These are companies that don't do knee-jerk reactions - no panic during recessions or pandemics, and no aggressive expansion during the halcyon times. They didn't panic during stormy periods, nor did they expand too aggressively during good times.

The key point here is making a clear, immovable decision on **how fast you want to grow.**

The only way you can really enjoy the journey is if you've got the vision, the foundations and the drive to propel you into a bright future with a steady, achievable growth goal in place.

Just how fast is your own scale-up journey? The challenge is the fact that there are too many companies that are encouraged to leap into high-growth mode, but are not prepared for what is to come. We're encouraged every day by government incentives, by media reports, but the simple truth is, many of us don't have the key things in place - to scale up appropriately and to enjoy doing so.

Follow your own path, don't be swayed by the growth journeys of others, or by incentives or press reports. **Everybody's growth journey is different.**

Set a pace that suits you. What's important is that you're growing, not stagnant. You're either growing or you're dying, but it's your choice, you're in control.

The 20-Mile March

Collins and Hansen devoted a chapter to the great story of the race to the South Pole in 1911/12. It's certainly worth covering, and I've always found it inspiring - with apologies to Captain Scott.

The challenge of who might reach the South Pole first came to a head in the famous tale of British explorer Robert Falcon Scott and Norwegian explorer Roald Amundsen, two experienced adventurers who believed they could reach the pole first, for national and personal glory, and of course, the incredible achievement.

While Amundsen had a few things in his favour, the main differentiator in his 1400 nautical mile, 99-day trek was his approach. He determined to try and achieve around 20 miles trekking every day, regardless of conditions. In good weather, 15 to 20 miles of trekking was achieved - never more. On bad days - with icy winds and poor visibility, his team trekked on, sometimes only covering a few miles, but still making headway.

Scott, on the other hand, pushed ahead regardless of good weather, exhausting his team. On bad weather days, Scott stayed put, frustrated, and huddled in his tent.

It comes as no surprise to us today that Amundsen's stoical approach led to victory. His team arrived at the South Pole some 33 days before Scott, proudly raising the Norwegian flag at the South Pole on 14 December 1911.

Captain Scott reached the South Pole on 17 January 1912. Scott's failure to get there first left him disappointed, and the tortuous return journey was never completed. Weak from exhaustion, hunger and extreme cold, his last diary entry is dated 29 March 1912. He died in his tent alongside two of his men.

While not a cheerful tale, the 20 Mile March concept is now widely quoted as a salutary lesson, akin to the tortoise and the hare, perhaps. The obvious question it leads us to is 'Are you Amundsen or Scott?' I know which I'd rather be!

As Jim Collins says: "10X business leaders in our research behaved very much like Amundsen."

> *"The 20-Mile March is more than a philosophy. It's about having concrete, clear, intelligent, and rigorously pursued performance mechanisms that keep you on track. The 20-Mile March creates two types of self-imposed discomfort: (1) the discomfort of unwavering commitment to high performance in difficult conditions, and (2) the discomfort of holding back in good conditions."*
> **-Jim Collins**

In his book 'The Last Place on Earth', author Roland Huntford identified that Amundsen and Scott had exactly the same ratio, (56%), of good days to bad days of weather. We can't, therefore, blame the environment for their success and failure - because they faced the same environment in the same year with the same goal. They saw very different outcomes mainly because they displayed very different behaviours.

If you're aiming for consistent performance, you need to understand both elements of a 20-Mile March: a lower and upper limit, a hurdle to jump over (*marching through sub-zero temperatures*) and a ceiling you won't rise above, (*marching twice as far in good weather*); the ambition to achieve, tempered by enough self-control to hold back.

Adopting a 20 Mile March approach helps by:

- Building confidence in your ability to perform well in adverse circumstances

- Reducing the likelihood of catastrophe when hit by disruption
- Helps you exert self-control in out-of-control environments.

What behavioural traits will you develop to ensure you enjoy the journey?

Think of the story of The Station to remember goals will never give you satisfaction - as soon as you hit one, there's another.

And remember the '20 Mile March' story to pace yourself, and remember the end goal remains achievable if you approach it with drive and commitment, vision and purpose.

While you can't control everything going on in the world, or perhaps even your own life, you can control your own 20 Mile March. So, tighten up your boots and get marching...!

Exercise: What's Your 20-Mile March?

Here are some questions to help you apply the idea to your business

What is the right upper limit that we should use to regulate our growth?

What do we already do that is consistent and successful that we might want to systemise?

Do we have a clear vision and long-term strategy that can guide our 20-mile march?

Carefully consider your answers, and write them down.

Forever Chasing Bubbles

Are you trying too hard?

Here's something that's probably happened to us all – a great analogy of how we can try too hard sometimes.

The other day I was trying to get a mass of dishwashing bubbles to go down the plughole in the sink.

The more I turned the taps on, the faster the mass of bubbles flew around the sink – but they just wouldn't go down the plughole. There was water splashing everywhere, I was getting frustrated, even angry, but still, there was no reward for my increased efforts (sound familiar?).

In the end, I switched the taps off - and all the bubbles sailed down the plughole!

The moral of the story is: It isn't always about effort, more pressure and trying hard. Sometimes we need to do the very opposite – and turn the pressure off.

Coaching Questions

What speed of growth will you aim for?

How much effort are you willing to put in, day after day after day, to reach your goals?

What do you enjoy most in life?

How much time would you like to devote to that aspect of your life, realistically?

How can you achieve that goal?

Are you ready for a long, slow, steady march to greatness?

How do you feel about things out of your control? We must accept that all businesses face continuous uncertainty and that we cannot control, or accurately predict, significant aspects of the world around us...

Do you accept full responsibility for the fate of your business?

CHAPTER 6

Strategy One: Develop the Right Habits

"Be undeniably good. No marketing effort or social media buzzword can be a substitute for that."
-Anthony Volodkin

"And once you understand that habits can change, you have the freedom and the responsibility to remake them."
-Charles Duhigg

"The difference between an amateur and a professional is in their habits. An amateur has amateur habits. A professional has professional habits. We can never free ourselves from habit. But we can replace bad habits with good ones."
-Steven Pressfield

A Chinese Proverb

I would like to share a Chinese proverb that goes something like this: "In our minds there are two Tigers that are continually fighting each other. One is the tiger of negativity, loss, despair and rejection, the other is the tiger of success, happiness, love and knowledge.

The question is – which one of the tigers will win?

The answer is – whichever one you choose to feed...

We need to talk about your habits, how to break them and how to make them. As a scale-up leader, it is your habits that will ultimately determine how successful you are.

Habits - at least, good habits - are crucial in scale-up leadership. We are what we repeatedly do. To achieve scale-up leadership, we often need to work towards being someone different.

As Henry Ford famously put it: "If you always do what you've always done, you'll always get what you've always got."

But firstly, what is a habit? Most people agree they are an acquired mode of behaviour that's become nearly or completely involuntary. In other words, a lot of stuff we do each and every day is habitual, even if we are unaware of the habit. From cleaning your teeth to driving, to eating certain foods at certain times of day, we all have long-ingrained habits. It's about taking behaviour and turning it into an automatic routine.

For the purposes of this chapter, it's useful to consider the words of author, lecturer and neuroscientist Joe Dispenza, who in his book "*Breaking the Habit of Being Yourself: How to Lose Your Mind and Create a New One*", wrote:

"*Psychologists tell us that by the time we're in our mid-30s, our identity or personality will be completely formed. This means that for those of us over 35, we have memorised a select set of behaviours, attitudes, beliefs, emotional reactions, habits, skills, associative memories, conditioned responses, and perceptions that are now subconsciously programmed within us.*

"*Those programs are running us because the body has become the mind. This means that we will think the same thoughts, feel the same feelings, react in identical ways, behave in the same manner, believe the same dogmas, and perceive reality the same ways."*

Dispenza also says that by midlife, 95 per cent of who we are is a series of subconscious 'programs' that are running automatically - like driving, worrying, complaining and feeling unhappy, to name a few.

Old Habits Create Future Problems...

Did you know that the space shuttle was designed by the Romans?!

On either side of the Space Shuttle are two massive solid rocket boosters (SRBs). The SRBs have to be shipped by train from the factory to the launch site.

The railroad line from the factory is on a railroad track that is 4 feet, 8.5 inches. So, the limit for the size of the solid rocket boosters was set by the width of the railway track.

But why is the track such a unique measurement?

Well, railroad tracks in the US are the same width in Britain, and American railroads were built by British immigrants.

Why did the British build them like that? Because the first rail lines were built by the same people who built the tramways before trains existed, and that's the gauge they used.

They used that measurement, because the people who built the tramways used the same jigs and tools that were used for building wagons which used that wheel spacing.

And why did the wagons have that particular odd wheel spacing?

Because if they tried to use any other spacing, the wagon wheels would break on some of the old, long-distance roads in England. You see, that was the spacing of the wheel ruts.

So, who built those old rutted roads? The first long distance roads across Europe (and England) were built by Imperial Rome for its armies.

The roads have been used ever since. And the ruts in the roads? Roman war chariots first formed the initial ruts, which everyone else had to match for fear of destroying their wagon wheels. The chariots were made for, or by, Imperial Rome, so they were all alike in the matter of wheel spacing.

This connection was first written about by an Irish solicitor named Bill Holohan, when he explained how 2,000 years earlier, the Romans set in place the restrictions for the size of the space shuttle.

(See Rich Litvin, [The opposite of a default future is a created life](#))

Exercise: Where Are You Trapped?

What ruts - or habits - are YOU trapped in, that were set in place years, or even generations, earlier?

Try asking your parents or grandparents about their beliefs and habits around money, love, intimacy or success. You may be surprised just how far back your habits and beliefs go.

Then the question arises...what are you going to do about that?

_____

_____

_____

A lot of these 'automatic' habits were formed early in life, when we didn't have the tools or resources to understand, react or respond in any other way. Habits are controlled by a certain part of the brain, the basal ganglia, which frees up the rest of the brain to concentrate on other things. In other words, mundane habits are *literally* happening automatically, while your brain efficiently delegates management of the task, freeing you up to use your brain for other more important things. Our conscious brains can only focus on one thing at a time - and habits allow this to happen.

Many of these ingrained habits are developed to protect ourselves, then they become a way of life.

Key to developing the right habits to succeed as a scale up leader is awareness of which habits serve you and which hinder your progress.

The habits which have got you where you are today aren't necessarily right for where you need to go.

You need to find who you need to become and what habits you need to develop in order to get there.

The challenge here of course, is that our ingrained habits are difficult to change.

Habits make neural pathways in your brain - which means they can almost become cemented in place. You can break a bad - or unwanted habit - by replacing it with a different habit. Science now knows that the brain is a lot more elastic than we used to think. 'Neuroplasticity' means we all have the ability to unlearn, re-learn and re-wire those neural pathways that dictate our habits and behaviours. And in order to break bad habits, we have to identify them.

Exercise: What Are Your Habits?

Identify your key habits - good and bad, from hitting the snooze button to that daily walk. List them, and consider which ones serve you, and which ones hinder you.

Name of habit	*How does it serve you?*

Button it Up

Do you know why men's shirts have buttons on the right but women's have them on the left?

For men, it was probably because that made it easier to reach a gun inside. Before guns, swordsmen needed jackets which buttoned left over right, so as not to catch the handle when they drew their sword.

For women, it was probably because when buttons were invented, in the 13th century, the woman wearing the shirt wasn't the person buttoning it — they had servants button their shirts.

Some people believe most women held babies with their left hands, so they needed their right hand to open their shirt buttons for breastfeeding.

I'm less interested in the correct historical reason for why we do our buttons on a particular side, than the fact that we do...

It's easier to replace a bad habit with a new behaviour, instead of just trying to erase the pattern altogether.

Habits involve a cue, a behaviour and a result. Quite often, the result of a habit leads to a dopamine rush - a 'happy pill' if you like - or a reward. Understanding and interrupting the loop of these three elements is key to breaking a habit, and creating new ones, as underlined by Charles Duhigg in his interesting book, *The Power of Habit.*

Duhigg says: "What we know from lab studies is that it's never too late to break a habit. Habits are malleable throughout your entire life. But we also know that the best way to change a habit is to understand its structure — that once you tell people about the cue and the reward and you force them to recognize what those factors are in a behaviour, it becomes much, much easier to change."

So, as we try to change a habit, it may take time and it's not a pleasant experience.

We generally view the idea of changing habits with reluctance.

Then, it's a struggle to maintain change as we create new habits. It's been suggested that a great time to change your habits is when you've had a change of routine - like on holiday, for instance. A time and place where you do not suffer from your usual cues and reference points. Why not try breaking a habit next time you take a holiday?

To change, we have to become aware of existing habits and then develop awareness and new ways of thinking - and constantly work on changing those habits.

I introduce my clients to three powerful strategies to employ when forming and maintaining new habits during my career. They are:

Micro Steps

Start small. You might be keen to go 'all-in' but the science shows that taking slow, small steps towards positive new behaviours (habits) works best.

As James Clear, author of "*Atomic Habits: An Easy & Proven Way to Build Good Habits & Break Bad Ones*," puts it: "The central idea is to create an environment where doing the right thing is as easy as possible. Much of the battle of building better habits comes down to finding ways to reduce the friction associated with our good habits."

Small wins drive us forward, and those small wins start to build into new habits.

Habit Stacking

Journalist Steve Scott, otherwise known as 'The Habits Guy', is credited with coining the term habit stacking. The theory goes that we can help build and stick with new habits by tapping into our brain's affinity with creating short-cuts by associating clusters of activity with each other.

So, by 'clustering' activities, or the habits you want to develop and maintain, there's a higher chance of remembering them by simply associating related tasks with each other.

For example, creating a morning routine involving taking vitamins, reading a chapter of a book and flossing your teeth would involve setting everything up that you need to do these activities the night before - then doing it every day for four to six weeks - then it becomes habitual activity.

Habit Compounding

Regular, small daily habits - things we might not necessarily initially enjoy - compound over time into tangible results. For example, ten minutes of meditation a day adds up to 3,640 minutes of meditation a year! Cycling just a kilometre a day means you'll do 365kms a year.

Make a decision to take tiny steps to move towards better habits today, and you'll soon start to reap the benefits of compounding.

So, we've established where habits come from, and what steps we can take to change negative or bad ones. Now, let's look at the habits that a scale-up leader needs.

Just before we dive into that, it's worth reading what habits we shouldn't carry with us, post-pandemic, in one of my recent blogs, here.

(https://www.hollyscherer.com/compounding-habits/)

The Ultimate Habit Breaker - Alcoholics Anonymous

There is no real science behind the famous 12 steps employed by AA. It's simply a means of encouraging people, in a supportive group, to break the habit and replace it with new ones. It gives people a new routine - meetings - rather than heading to the pub. As Duhigg puts it in The Power of Habit: "At some point, if you're changing a really deep-seated behaviour, you're going to have a moment of weakness. And at that moment, if you can look across a room and think, 'Jim's kind of a moron. I think I'm smarter than Jim. But Jim has been sober for three years. And if Jim can do it, I can definitely do it,' that's enormously powerful."

Awareness of self is an important aspect of your habit-breaking journey. Think about who you want to become? Who do you admire as a leader? Investigate what traits and habits they display. Think about your most successful moments and your least successful.

You can define who you need - or want - to become.

It's entirely possible that you're about to become a very different leader to who you were previously. So, you need to shift your conscious state and identify those habits and patterns that serve or do not serve you.

What habits must you stop doing? Which must you start doing?

The Habits to Master as a Scale-Up Leader

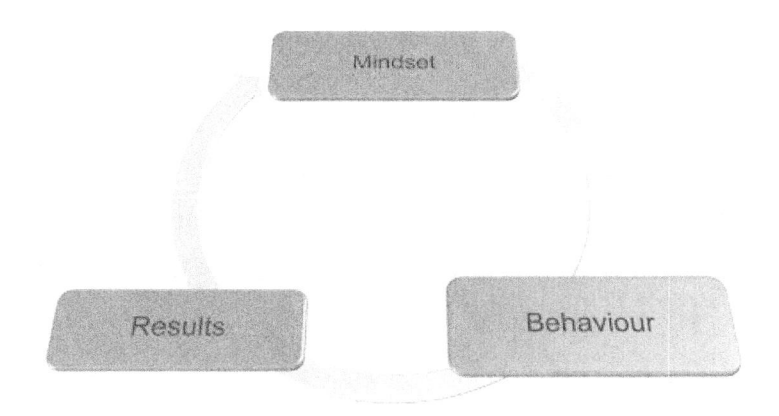

There are three areas of habits which have a disproportionate impact on your success as a scale up leader here, which all leaders must continuously master - **mindset, energy management and time management**.

Mindset

Our mindset is concerned with mental aptitude and inclination. Every day, you need to make sure you've got a positive mindset which is in tune with where you want to go.

Your Mindset Determines Your Behaviour

And it's our behaviour that helps produce results.

So, if you're getting effective results from those you're leading, you know you're having a positive impact on them, and therefore yourself, and the whole thing cycles up very quickly.

But when you show up with a negative mindset, you display behaviours that don't necessarily support you, so you don't feel great and you get negative results - which therefore reinforces a negative mindset.

The whole thing snowballs and cycles down very quickly.

So, you must focus every day on getting that positive mindset, which is driving you forwards.

For the last 15 years or more, I've been focusing on exactly what that mindset is, and how to get that mindset in the morning.

There are certain things you need to go through, which I have found through trial and learning over the last 15 years. These have been brilliantly summarized by a guy called Hal Elrod, in his book, *The Miracle Morning.*

If you look at the habits you need to make sure you've got 'built-in', and you look at all the successful people out there - whether they're business people, actors or politicians - Elrod says there are certain things they do religiously Every. Single. Day. These are easily remembered by the acronym SAVERS.

SAVERS stands for Silence, Affirmations, Visualisation, Exercise, Reading and Scribing.

Spend 60 minutes every morning going through the SAVERS and you will develop rock solid, positive habits that have been proven to help us grow in life.

First up, **Silence**. Get comfortable - by silence, we mean meditation, some sort of contemplation. This is useful quiet time with yourself, a period where you connect with yourself. Help yourself out by choosing a meditation app.

Secondly, **Affirmations**. What affirmations do you need to be saying to yourself which will help you go and rewire your brain, rewire your habits and improve the belief that you've become an excellent scale-up leader? Elrod suggests repeating your affirmation daily, ideally out loud. "They immediately make an impression on your subconscious mind," he explains in his book. "They transform how you think and feel so you can overcome your limiting beliefs and behaviours and replace them with those you need to succeed."

Thirdly, **Visualisation**. So, this means visualising where you want to be, what you want to become, creating that mental picture, and focusing on how you feel when you think that through. Elrod suggests you should "visualise living your ideal day, performing all tasks with ease, confidence and enjoyment."

Next up, **Exercise**. We all know this affects the mind, body and soul in nothing but positive ways. Whether it's a brief yoga session or a walk around the block, fitting in exercise sets you up in a better mental place to face the challenges of the day.

Then some sort of **Reading**. In my case, I spend my time catching up on the latest management thoughts and practices. Self-help over news, here, as news can affect your mindset. Management, health, nutrition, love, spirituality, exercise.... all of these topics should be on your miracle morning reading list. Aim for just ten pages a day.

Finally, some sort of **Scribing** or journaling. Just start writing. Write your thoughts and feelings. Don't worry about grammar, structure or coherence - the important thing is to undertake the mind-freeing exercise of simply putting pen to paper (or fingers to keyboard!).

Those are habits you need to make sure you do every morning. SAVERS will enable a positive mindset every day.

Energy Management

Let's not pretend being a scale-up leader won't take your energy. So, we need to be in a position where management of your energy - always a finite resource - is an ingrained habit.

You're driven, you're excited, keen and ready to push yourself and your team through this incredible period of rapid scale-up, right?

But wait - pushing yourself relentlessly leads to health issues. Certainly, in the last few years - with the cloud of COVID-19 hanging over us all - I've seen more executives suffering from burnout. They've been operating under the misconception that working harder and longer through the pandemic will ensure company survival.

Compare this to how top athletes behave. They train in bursts, performing at their absolute best for just 10% of their time.

For the rest of their time, they know the value of disengaging, recuperating and re-energising, ready for their next competition or event.

As business leaders, our balance is wrong. Energy management, simply put, involves taking time each and every day to recuperate and re-energise.

If you examine typical human energy rhythms you have what's called circadian and ultradian rhythms. Circadian rhythms are those which occur every 24 hours - such as sleeping at night and being awake during the day.

Ultradian rhythms are those that occur more frequently in a 24-hour period and can last for 90 to 120 minutes, depending on the individual. An ultradian rhythm might be something like an individual sleep cycle.

These ultradian rhythms affect nearly all aspects of our physical, mental, and emotional well-being. They also play a big role in our "willpower" and our ability to carry out decisions.

ULTRADIAN PERFORMANCE RHYTHM

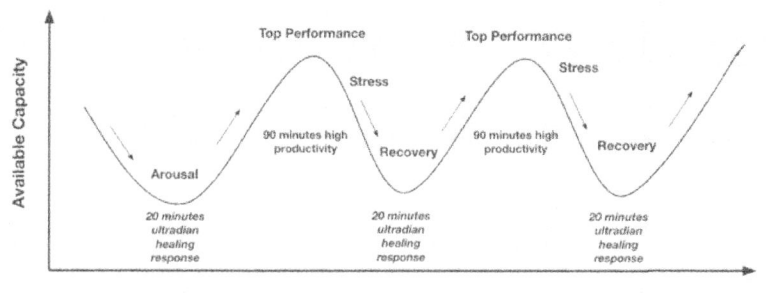

Adapted from The 20 Minute Break by Ernest L Rossi (Tarcher Putnam, 1991)

Think of ultradian rhythms as biological patterns that come hardwired into our DNA. You might call them the 'clock genes' if you like. They dictate how our bodies function over time. We must maintain our ultradian rhythms so our bodies function properly.

Your ultradian rhythms affect your daily activity.

First thing, you have mental focus and get into a flow of sustained activity. So, your body and brain burn through your supply of oxygen, glucose, and other energetic fuels.

After about 90 minutes, research suggests we reach the apex of productivity, entering what's known as an "ultradian performance peak."

Meanwhile, by-products of your mental and physical activity — metabolic waste, snippets of data, cellular debris — are building up in your system.

So, at around the 90-minute mark, this accumulation of (toxic) detritus manifests itself in the body as stress. Performance and productivity start to dip as your body enters what's known as an "ultradian trough"— a low point for your energy.

Recognise these feelings? Fatigue, grogginess, irritability, inability to concentrate, hunger, or fidgeting?

All effects of an ultradian trough - which leads to cravings for sugar, coffee, a cigarette, or carbs. You might wonder how you'll make it through the day, right?

Don't ignore these feelings. They're not negative. They're a sure sign that your body is functioning exactly as it should - so pay attention. And your body is calling for a break!

Take a break, recoup, regather your energy, walk around. Ideally, take 20 minutes to sort, file and cogitate over what you've been dealing with for the last few hours.

Having allowed yourself time to undergo the "ultradian healing response," you will feel fighting fit and ready for another couple of hours of high performing scale-up leadership!

It's natural to take a break every few hours, and again, studies have shown that those who take breaks like this perform consistently better, feel better and enjoy longer good health.

Ignore your body's messages for long enough, and the feeling of requiring a break may pass, but you simply won't perform as well. Tiredness leads to mistakes, after all.

Carry on pushing yourself all day, every day, and the law of diminishing returns kicks in – or rather, you put in more effort, but get less results.

Accepting and understanding that taking breaks leads to higher performance is most definitely a key habit for a scale-up leader to adopt. An inspirational scale-up leader will be seen taking breaks.

In the modern workplace, the concept of putting in longer hours to get the job done has backfired. People are becoming exhausted, disengaged and sick - then choosing a healthier work environment.

In a Harvard Business Review paper, "Manage your Energy, Not your Time," by Tony Schwartz and Catherine McCarthy, the authors talk about adopting certain practices every day to renew your 'four dimensions' of personal energy - physical, emotional, mental and spiritual.

In brief, they recommend a host of activities such as setting regular sleep hours, exercise, focusing in on tasks you enjoy, taking regular breaks, looking at issues through others' eyes and performing high-concentration tasks away from the distraction of phones and email.

This long list of daily rituals can quickly and easily turn to habits.

Your energy will hit peaks and troughs, and these needs analysing and managing, too. You'll have days - or even weeks - when you are more energetic, naturally. Remember the painter [Van Gogh](#) was only productive for a decade - but produced an enormous body of work during that time. Paying heed to these cycles reaps dividends - and remember, taking holidays every quarter is vital if you are to maintain solid momentum and protect your mental and physical health.

Time Management

Time management, of course, dovetails beautifully with energy management. Forming solid habits around how you spend your time - and with who, doing what, is a crucial aspect in your journey towards strong scale-up leadership.

Good time management habits might include scheduling the work you'd like to get done within a specific time frame. Be specific - write down what, where and when you want to do. Have a plan for your day, your week and month. Even larger plans for the year. If everything is mapped out, it's obviously easier to better manage your time.

You probably already know all too well that planning works. But how many of us take the time to plan our time? So today, try turning all your important tasks into schedules. Make appointments with your tasks - so you'll never miss completing them.

Equally - continuing my theme of enjoying the journey - schedule time for exercise, for relaxation, with family and with friends.

There are certain myths surrounding time management which I explored in a blog on my website some time ago. These include the fact that if you managed your time better you could 'do it all'. This is just not true. Admit you can't do everything, and evaluate where cuts can be made.

Also, there isn't one perfect time management system out there, rather a number of systems that can be studied and adapted for our own needs.

My third point in the blog is that you can't learn time management in a day, it takes study, evaluation and practice - for three months or more. Remember, changing habits takes time.

Finally, many of us believe we're hopeless at time management. That's not the case, it's simply another skill that can be developed and added to your suite of growing good management skills.

I've been helping leaders develop good time management skills for more than a decade now, so here are some basic, brief time management tips for you to get started:

1. **Start your day with planning**

    Setting your mind, your diary, priorities and goals on awakening gives you clarity, purpose and avoids wasting time on unnecessary tasks. Add in the Rule of 3 - that each day, you should only focus on three outcomes you want to achieve that day. Getting this day plan as a habit will work wonders - and future you will thank you.

2. **Start work at the same time every day**

    This might be a given, but set a time in stone, and you help your mindset itself into 'productivity mode'. This has become even more important in recent times with the rise of people working from home. Having the self-discipline to start at the same time, regardless of location, leads to greater satisfaction and productivity. Some have described the 'default diary' as the single most powerful time management tool available. And it's simple. With a 'default diary' you book in blocks of time in your diary to perform certain tasks at certain times, every day. This helps avoid tasks backing up.

3. **Use a timer during your work day**

    Knowing where your time goes is a key to unlocking more productivity. A timer helps you lock in those all-important breaks, and brings greater clarity and focus. Timing is good, but it's also worth tracking your activity. You begin to quickly see patterns. Most modern phones have a timer, but take a moment to check out all the apps and tools online with timing elements.

4. **Keep a 'to-do' list**

   Accept you can't remember everything. And no-one expects you to. A list provides clarity and focus, and allows us to gain the satisfaction of crossing off completed tasks. At the end of each day, check over the list and if there are any unfinished tasks, ask yourself why it wasn't completed, and give it priority on the next day's to-do list. Remember it's best to capture everything in one place, rather than sticky notes or scraps of paper all over the place!

5. **Eat the frog**

   "If it's your job to eat a frog, it's best to do it first thing in the morning. And if it's your job to eat two frogs, it's best to eat the biggest one first."
   -Mark Twain

   Productivity consultant Brian Tracy coined the phrase 'eat the frog', inspired by the above Mark Twain quote. I certainly find it an extremely powerful tool - get into the habit of doing the thing you want to do least, first. Starting off your day by completing the thing you've been putting off, dreading, or feeling uncomfortable with, is a great empowering action. By doing this, you're breaking the cycle of procrastination, creating positive momentum and great motivation to attack all your other tasks.

6. **The 80:20 Rule**

   The Pareto Principle - the 80/20 rule, states that 80% of our results come from 20% of our efforts. Applied in productivity and time management terms, you need to identify what's taking up your time, how you spend your day, and how those activities affect results. Once you've identified whether 20% of your effort does generate 80% of your results, it makes sense that you should prioritise and aim to improve on that 20%.

7. **F.O.C.U.S**

   I'll end this section with a great acronym - FOCUS - which stands for Follow One Course Until Successful. In other words, focus your attention with great attention until the task is done. The 'course' you are following might be a short-term goal, a meeting, or a pitch, for example. Equally, it could be to focus on your long-term goal, your vision, your North Star. The important thing is to learn how to focus, distraction free, until your task is done. If you focus on one key project, you'll achieve results much faster than trying to juggle multiple projects at once.

And don't forget - learning all these new habits will have a massively positive effect on you, your life and your productivity levels - so don't forget to enjoy the journey.

Coaching Questions

What is a scale up leader to you? Who do you need to become?

To become a scale up leader - what habits must you start, stop and continue?

How can you improve your time management skills?

How can you improve your energy throughout the day?

Do your morning and evening routines leave you energised and focused through the day? What must you change?

CHAPTER 7

Strategy Two: First Who, Then What

"If everyone is moving forward together then success takes care of itself."
-**Henry Ford**

"Find a group of people who challenge and inspire you, spend a lot of time with them, and it will change your life."
Amy Poehler

"The old adage "People are your most important asset" turns out to be wrong. People are not your most important asset. The right people are."
-**Jim Collins**

In this chapter, we'll take a deep dive into who you need to have alongside you on your scale-up journey.

It's not about defining what you need to do, rather it's about making sure you've got the right individuals and the right team around you.

These are the people who, first and foremost, enable you to take your business to a new level.

Recognise that the team that got you to this point in your business journey won't necessarily be the right people to take you to the next stage.

Remember, great companies recruit and secure the best talent ahead of making any major changes. You must build a great leadership team *before* defining and implementing your scale-up strategy.

I've mentioned Jim Collins' book, [Good To Great](), previously, but in it, he talks about whether we should position ourselves as a leadership *team*; a *group* of equals pushing towards a common goal. Or, alternatively, positioning yourself as an *individual* (visionary) leader, choosing to surround yourself with people who can help push your vision into reality.

Collins suggests that a great team extends beyond the workplace - your team should probably develop a sense of closeness, of comradeship, that extends beyond working hours. A great team understands each other's motivations, personal goals, strengths and weaknesses, for example. These are the traits of a high-performance team - where the team is judged by its results - rather than on individual results or efforts.

And your personal relationships matter too. Who you spend time with affects who you become.

As Tony Robbins famously said: "**Who you spend time with is who you become.**"

As a scale-up leader, you need to up your game - including who you mix with, for example.

You need to BE the person who delivers the vision. You need to have supporters around you who inspire you, rather than people that will pull you down.

Choose Who You Spend Time With

There are a number of people who have stepped outside their normal circles to help them become the people they need to be.

Think of the British Olympic runner Mo Farah training with East Africans in Kenya and Ethiopia, British tennis star and double Wimbledon champion Andy Murray forgoing training in the UK to train in the US, and Steve Jobs mentoring Tim Cook at Apple...the point here is that these people, who were already considered to be at the top of their game, went to extra lengths to gain new skills outside of the norms.

The second key point here is that as you scale your business you need to have the right team around you.

There's lots of research out there, some of it surprising - like your income is generally the average income of your five closest friends outside of your family - perhaps a twist on motivational speaker *Jim Rohn's* famous words: "You are the average of the five people you spend the most time with."

In *The Compound Effect*, Darren Hardy wrote: "According to research by social psychologist Dr. David McClelland of Harvard, [the people you habitually associate with] determine as much as 95 percent of your success or failure in life."

Now it might be harsh, or shocking to you to read this, but it might be time to consider who you spend your leisure time with, as well as analysing who you turn to for business advice, and who your closest confidante in the company is.

Exercise: Write a quick list of your top five:

Friends

_____
_____
_____
_____
_____

Influencers

_____
_____
_____
_____
_____

Authors

_____
_____
_____
_____
_____

Business advisors

_____
_____
_____
_____
_____

Exercise: Spend Time with the Energisers…

The following grid looks at who you spend most time with on two dimensions. It examines whether those individuals are a positive or negative influence and whether they are more takers than givers when you interact with them. From your list above, consider who you spend most time with. Categorise them across the dimensions and quadrants shown in the grid below.

When you've completed it, reflect on:

How can I reduce the time I spend with Sappers?

How can I spend more time with Energisers?

How can I educate those people in the Poor Me and Groupies sections to become Energisers?

While they may even be the same people, analyse your list and decide who among them will really help you become a successful scale-up leader.

We're not saying throw your life-long friendships away; but simply decide who it is good to spend more time with at this stage in your scale-up journey.

REVIEW.....

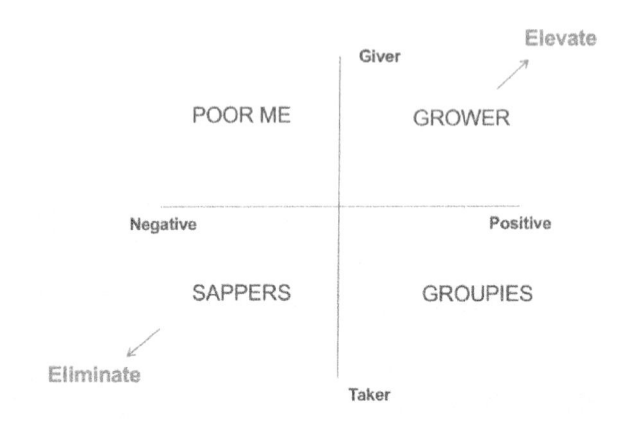

	Giver	Elevate ↗
Negative	POOR ME	GROWER
	SAPPERS	GROUPIES Positive
↙ Eliminate		
	Taker	

Why does who we spend our time with matter so much? The short answer is it can dramatically change the way we view the world and the way we act within the world. The idea is that you surround yourself with positive and inspirational people, and who doesn't want that?

Another brief exercise is to spend a moment thinking who would you like within your circle? Who would you like to hear speaking in the next year? Think of 25 people who might help you get further, faster.

In my case, as a younger business coach and consultant, my own list included luminaries in the field like Brendon Burchard, Seth Godin, Tony Robbins, Vishen Lakhiani and Lisa Nichols, alongside many others.

Today, I have reached out to them all, and know them all.

Perhaps you might say, "let's not have idols", but rather, simply reach out to the people you most admire"

And:

"And remember: If no-one is inspiring you, you're the inspiration."

While the digital realm has allowed us to converse with people who might previously have been unreachable, if you can't make contact with those you most admire directly, you can still learn from them.

Devour their books, watch their YouTube channel, read their blogs - take a little time to immerse yourself in their world and their thinking.

And remember: If no-one is inspiring you, you're the inspiration

Getting the Right People on the Bus

Image by OpenClipart-Vectors on Pixabay

If you think of your business as a bus, who's on the bus? Are they all happy to head in the same direction, to the ultimate destination? As I said earlier - the team that got you to this level might not be the team to get you to the next. Fresh people bring fresh ideas, and new inspiration. While some people hold us back, others push us forwards.

Some of your old team may have worked hard, and given their all, but might no longer be truly aligned with your passion and direction.

It's tough, and often will involve personal conflict, but as a scale up leader you must decide who to take with you on the journey. The important factor to bear in mind is simply what percentage of key seats are filled with the right people?

Ask yourself if there's a role for those people in your business moving forwards. Can they grow in their roles, and/or as individuals at the pace you need them to achieve your desired growth?

To accelerate growth, you need to put the best people possible in place. Ultimately you want people that are so reliable, so good at what they do, that you are effectively putting yourself out of a job!

> *"Great vision without great people is irrelevant."*
> **-Jim Collins**

There are several key questions you might ask potential new employees, not least of which is that past performance is a great indicator of future performance. Have they got relevant experience? Have they worked in a scale-up environment previously? You can't afford to settle for average. And always look to upgrade your talent.

Of course, the environment has to be good, too. You need to ensure, having found the right talent, that they can operate to their full potential in your business.

To align with your values and your company culture, your shiny new talent must *understand* and be able to live that culture and values.

Of course, the elephant in the room here - or perhaps, on the bus - is salary. Don't skimp on salary. Whether we admit it or not, most of us, to some extent, are driven and motivated by money. Pay as much as you can afford to get the best talent on board.

However, there's a great note here. The right people will do everything to help build a great company, *not* because of what they will "get" for it, but because they cannot imagine settling for anything less.

As Collins puts it: "Their moral code requires building excellence for its own sake, and you're no more likely to change that with a compensation package than you're likely to affect whether they breathe."

Simply put, he believes that the right people will do the right things and deliver the best results they're capable of, regardless of any incentives.

Compensation is important, but for very different reasons in your successful scale-up company. The purpose of compensation should not be to get the right behaviours from the wrong people, but to get the right people on the bus in the first place - and to keep them there.

So, you've found your 'Who'. The dream team that gets you, understands your company culture and goals, and has the right fit and energy to help you scale-up.

Now What?

If you recall, this chapter is entitled 'First Who, Then What". We've covered the who, so now let's look at the 'what'.

This encapsulates what your strategy is, and how you will keep your star team on course, and motivated.

The idea is to get the right people on the bus, and then set your destination together.

As Collins suggests, starting with "who," rather than "what," puts you in a stronger position to quickly adapt to the ever-changing world.

If your people are on the bus because of where it is going, what happens when you need to change direction? That's a problem. Your team needs to be cohesive, and want to be part of the team because of who else is on board. And that makes it easier to change direction, especially if that change of direction leads to mutually agreed and understood success.

The right people negate the need for you to motivate and manage them - they'll be self-motivated, enjoying the chance to produce results and be a part of creating something awesome.

Having the wrong people, but the right direction, simply means you'll never have a great company.

When your talent starts working as a team, you need to deliver the 'whats'. What is your strategy? How are you going to deliver your vision, and ensure everyone has bought into that vision?

What your vision is clearly helps define where you want, and need to go.

Bear in mind, especially as evidenced by the pandemic, that sometimes the best laid strategies change. You need a team that's highly flexible and willing to change. While your ultimate vision may not change, the strategy on how to get there may well do so. Aim for you and your team to work with agility, flexibility and develop different possible pathways towards achievement of your end goals.

What remains true, despite a rapidly changing world, and important, is laying out a clearly defined and understood strategy, while ensuring you are learning as an individual and as an organisation faster than your competitors and faster than the marketplace.

Coaching Questions

Do you have the right people around to support you becoming a scale up leader?

What are the 25 relationships you must cultivate to go further faster?

How must you change to attract the right people into your life?

How might other people (with a different personality from you) approach this situation?

If you were to start your business again today, would you recruit the same team?

Do your key team see their roles as a job or a responsibility?

CHAPTER 8

Strategy Three: Letting Go

> *"Letting go means to come to the realization that some people are a part of your history, but not a part of your destiny."*
> -Steve Maraboli

> *"We must be willing to let go of the life we have planned, so as to have the life that is waiting for us."*
> -E. M. Forster

A Tragedy with a Strong Message

In 1949, thirteen of sixteen men died battling a relatively small blaze that turned deadly in Mann Gulch, Montana. Upon investigating why most of the 'smokejumpers' (firefighters who parachute in to fight fires) died, while just three lived, author Norman Maclean found some startling facts.

Mann Gulch is surrounded by steep canyon walls. When the wind turned on the smokejumpers, they were in a race with the fire up those steep walls. Unexpectedly, the fire started to spread much faster than anticipated.

One of the amazing things Maclean discovered was that the thirteen who died had carried their tools - heavy poleaxes, saws, shovels - all in very heavy backpacks - while attempting to outrun the fire up those steep walls.

In other words, the thirteen had run as far as they could with all their equipment, even though that equipment was useless in a race with the fire. Their inability to drop their equipment ultimately prevented them from outrunning the fire.

To the brave firefighters, their tools were more than simple objects - they represented who they were, why they were there and what they were trained to do. Dropping their tools meant abandoning their existing knowledge, training and experience.

This might not seem like a hard choice to make, but because they hadn't been trained for such a moment, they had no alternative models for behaviour. In moments of uncertainty and danger, clinging to the old "right" way might seem like a good idea, but it is usually deadly.

The three survivors thought outside of the box, using alternative methods of escaping the fire.

Once they figured out they were no longer fighting the fire, but trying to escape from it, they realized they had to drop all their equipment. One survivor used a technique called the 'escape fire' where he took a match and lit a 'ring' around himself so that the fire would "jump" over him. When he tried to suggest it to the other men, they continued running up the steep slope because the 'escape fire' technique had not been part of their training.

The question is this: What are the poleaxes, shovels and backpacks you're running with? What are the tired, worn-out strategies and tools you are lugging around? What existing models of behaviour do you need to drop? What existing knowledge, training or experience needs to be abandoned?

People who learn the critical business skills and tools necessary to survive and thrive will be the winners. Survivors and successful people are always learning and practicing to improve their game. New circumstances always require new skills and tools - the alternative is suffering and death.

That extremely harsh lesson delivers a blunt message - learn to let go. The old ways might be good, but they don't always remain right. By learning to 'let go' of old habits, we are creating time to scale, and focus on new opportunities - while not being distracted by shiny new toys.

Charles Darwin is famous for his 'Survival of the Fittest' theory. But what's interesting here to us is his definition of "fittest." It is not the biggest, fastest, strongest or smartest. It is the most *adaptable*.

The species that survive are the ones which are flexible. And flexibility comes with learning the ability to let go - that is, let go of old work habits and ways of working.

So, key to growth is adapting strategies to fit changing circumstances - competition, consumer preferences or interest rates, for example.

Flexibility requires that you know where you are and what is, or isn't, working.

Experience tells us the only constant in business is change. You could have made millions between 1996 and 2000 by waking up every morning and buying every "dotcom" listed on the stock market. Like all ideas, that was a great one until it wasn't. What caused it to go from a great idea to a bad idea was simply a change in the environment.

Being aware of, prepared for and willing to adapt to any one of a number of changes is a key facet of any scale-up leader.

And letting go might take work. Think of yourself as an old, slow, overloaded computer. There's a drive full of work, images, music, video and old, unused software. It works, and familiarity might keep you attached to it, but de-clutter and re-organise the computer's drive and it breathes new life into the machine. Those old, outdated programs and files are holding you back in your productivity; just like old, outdated ideas. Some people even have one laptop purely for writing, and another, more powerful desktop machine for internet use, for example.

Are you going to be an outdated computer, or a super-fast, future-ready machine?

Exercise: What Areas Require Change?

Write down your answers to these questions:

Where are you sticking to answers which were right, but in a different environment?

_____

_____

Which part of your company needs to adapt to the realities of today's environment?

_____

_____

Which strategies got you here - but will not make a difference today?

_____

_____

What practices are now obsolete or irrelevant?

_____

_____

What question(s) do you need to ask to rekindle the growth and profitability of your business?

_____

_____

Let Go by Saying No!

A drain of time for most of us is doing things we commit to out of obligation, unassertiveness, or just not properly considering how much time they will take.

Why would you stick with old habits that no longer serve you? How many of us do this? Do you really need to attend those meetings, be involved with those reports or be on that call? These are all regular tasks that can drain our time, energy and perhaps even motivation without us even noticing...so learn to say no, like Warren Buffet.

Sometimes it's easy to say "yes" impulsively just to feel like we've answered the email and checked it off our list.

Remember, as your success increases, requests (and opportunities) from others also increase. And taking on too much leads to stress, frustration and ineffectiveness.

Successful people know how to create time for opportunities that serve their highest priorities, versus sticking to commitments and old habits.

Sometimes, that means disappointing other people - but this is easier to do if you give yourself permission to be "good enough", rather than perfect.

> *"Your success is determined more by what you say no to than what you say yes to."*
> **-Stuart Ross**

Focus - as previously mentioned - means you develop a good new habit of saying no to certain tasks to allow people or the company to be more successful, by honing in with razor-like focus on certain goals, aims or tasks.

How to Avoid "Shiny Toy" Syndrome...

We all know how easy it is to get distracted from your goals and plans. Abandoning an ongoing project in favour of a new distraction is a sure-fire way to ruin your business - and never hit those goals.

This is known as "shiny toy" syndrome. You're always seeking the newest, latest, greatest thing - but it only offers fleeting happiness.

I see this as the number one challenge in stopping successful entrepreneurs from realising their potential.

To generate focus, and avoid jumping head first into new projects, while taking your eyes off the (long-term) prize, there are techniques I've found helpful in evaluating new opportunities.

Postpone Your Decision. Before allowing the excitement of the new to consume you, wait a few days. Then, after this pause, re-consider your decision as to whether or not to commit to the new opportunity. My experience has seen people's enthusiasm often wanes after a few days' self-reflection. It also empowers you to better evaluate whether the new project pushes you closer to your goal.

Use a Review Board. Seek the knowledge and skills of those around you. Get input from your team, and see if they buy in to the idea. A good team will feel empowered to reveal their true opinions, and those opinions might be that undertaking a new project could endanger a more important existing goal. If you don't have a team, create your own *review board*. Ask those you trust for their input before committing to new projects.

Forced Choice Technique. List everything you want to do. Then prioritise that list using a 'forced comparison' - compare items one at a time, from top to bottom. Start by asking which you would rather do – item 1 or item 2. Take the winner and compare it to the next item on the list. Then compare that winner – let's say item 3 – and compare it to item 4. By going through the list, you'll identify your number-one priority, and provide yourself with good focus. Repeat the exercise until there's one priority.

After this process, ask yourself: "What is the most effective use of my time now?" and "What's the most important thing to do today?" This will help you maintain focus among myriad choices.

(For more detail on these tips, see Jack Canfield's blog, [Beat the "Shiny Object" Syndrome](#))

Find What's Important

The legendary business guru, Steve Jobs, famously brought Apple back from the brink of failure after doing one simple thing: he reduced the number of products.

Richard Rumelt, a business strategist, discussed Jobs' bold manoeuvre in his book, **Good Strategy/Bad Strategy**: "Within a year, things changed radically at Apple. Although many observers had expected Jobs to rev up the development of advanced products, or engineer a deal with Sun, he did neither. What he did was both obvious and, at the same time, unexpected. He shrunk Apple to a scale and scope suitable to the reality of its being a niche producer in the highly competitive personal computer business. He cut Apple back to a core that could survive."

Jobs clearly understood that only a few of its (then) overly wide range of products were making a profit. So, he simply retained those products and stopped manufacturing the loss makers. Most of the inventory was loss-making at that time, so he reduced the number of distributors, too.

This bold, yet simple and decisive move saved Apple, and gave it renewed focus and energy.

We all need to be more like Jobs. Focusing on just two or three initiatives or growth concepts helps retain focus - remember, if you try to make everything a priority, nothing is a priority.

Letting go involves some soul searching, some business analysis and a great deal of confidence. Letting go is a crucial step in the scale-up journey, and while it shouldn't be taken lightly, once you feel like you're ready to let go of old ideas, old practices and thinking, it's time to embrace the next step...

Coaching Questions

What habits are not supportive of where you want to go?

If you were to have this day again, what would you have done differently, knowing what you know now?

What 'shiny toys' are distractions to your being productive?

What can you delegate to others?

What's preventing you from delegating?

How will you address the barriers to delegation?

CHAPTER 9

Strategy Four: Live in the Future, but be Present in the Now

> "Vision is the art of seeing what is invisible to others."
> -**Jonathan Swift**

> "Vision is the true creative rhythm."
> -**Robert Delaunay**

> "Good business leaders create a vision, articulate the vision, passionately own the vision, and relentlessly drive it to completion."
> -**Jack Welch**

This chapter is another step on the journey to scale-up leadership success, and involves more looking inside, and more reflection, coupled with bold, external action. You need to be living firmly in the now, but living as if your future vision is a reality.

Your path will be beset by problems, by challenges, and yes, even some failures. You need to learn how to operate a fine balance between now and the future.

While tackling day-to-day problems head on, you equally need to anchor yourself in the future with a powerful vision of where you want to be.

Being Present in the Now

Most of us live in the past or the future. We dream of past successes, and of a bright future. But few of us rarely dwell in the present. We all need to work on being literally present in the moment - addressing our current reality and the problems it can often bring.

According to Keith Cunningham, a foremost authority on business mastery, the 'problems' most of us are dealing with are not really the actual problems.

So, let's do some work to identify what the real problems are.

Keith Cunningham explains how everyone has a way they think something "is". According to the business expert, the problem most people have is they are *not particularly honest* about the reality of their situation.

For example, we may sugar-coat things or tell ourselves something isn't so bad. How honest are you? With yourself, and with others?

We all know the truth is what sets us free.

As long as we are lying to ourselves or not telling the truth, we don't have the opportunity to make a change.

At the same time, we also have an opinion on the way things "ought" to be, or, at least, the way we would like them to be. And most of us are experts on this. We have clarity on the way we would like the future to look.

When we are asked what the problem is, we normally describe the gap between what "is" and what "ought" to be. In reality, that isn't the problem. That's a symptom. We need to understand what's truly blocking our progress. The *symptom* indicates something is wrong, but does not shed light on what's causing it.

For example, if someone is 10 pounds overweight, if they identify the problem as being 10 pounds overweight, what they will conclude is maybe they should buy exercise equipment, buy some health books, join a gym, or get a personal trainer. But here, weight gain is a symptom of something else in life - an underlying illness, an eating disorder, a life without enough exercise, eating at wrong times or comfort eating - the list of potential problems which cause weight gain is enormous. Treating it tactically (with a gym membership, for example) might help lose weight, but it doesn't necessarily treat the underlying problem.

We identify the 'gap', (between where we are and where we want to be), call it the problem (*when in reality it is a symptom*), and we're highly tactical in our response, which sabotages our results.

As Keith says: "The higher you want to go, the greater the requirement to have people around you who will tell you the truth. You need people around you who will see what you're doing and who will give you advice, and then you gotta be willing to hear the advice. As long as we are arrogant or unwilling to listen, it does no good to ask."

Now, rethink the problem you wrote down. Is it REALLY the problem? Is it the core root underlying problem blocking your forward progress? OR... is there something buried below it that you have to figure out?

Living in the Future: Eyes on the Prize

There's something people have noticed that a number of visionary leaders share - living as if they've achieved their compelling idea. It's as if they're living in the future; a future of their own design, where their current vision is manifested.

Take five minutes to listen to Elon Musk discussing his Space X plans. What grabs you? He talks with passion, confidence, and unshakeable belief. He's living in the future, where Space X is delivering on its amazing promise of making life multiplanetary.

POWER OF A COMPELLING VISION

Belief → Potential → Action → Results → (Belief)

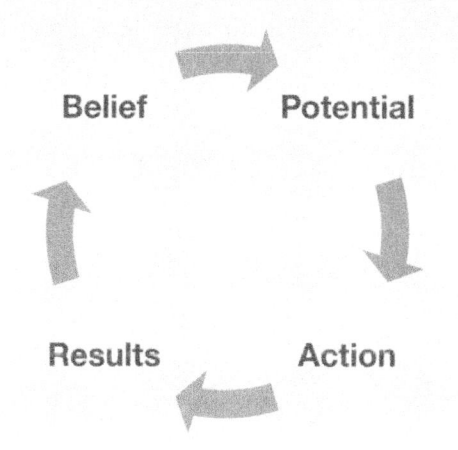

The diagram above is pretty self-explanatory - perhaps best exemplified in the short phrase 'walk the talk'. Every organisation has a certain amount of potential.

Individuals within the organisation take action to manifest that potential. That action leads to results, which influence the belief as an organisation.

It's a cycle.

But depending on the level of belief, the organisation is either going to increase or decrease its potential. If potential increases, they're taking more action, and they get bigger results, increase their beliefs, and the whole cycle goes up very quickly.

But the danger is that the cycle will go down.

So, when you believe the organisation has great potential, but action doesn't lead to the result you want or expect, your belief in yourself and the organisation drops. And then the whole thing can snowball down very quickly until you do just enough to get by - and that's where the power of a compelling vision comes in:

POWER OF A COMPELLING VISION

Belief → Potential

Vision

Results ← Action

Vision is what keeps the other elements in the circle alive. If a company achieves bad results, levels of belief drop, the potential drops and less action is taken.

Alternatively, if a charismatic leader has bold faith in the vision, it will pull everyone through the bad times (note Steve Jobs' Apple turnaround in the last chapter). Think of Henry Ford, of Jack Welch, of Elon Musk - all bold, visionary leaders, who drove/drive their companies to great heights.

We all need to master the ability to visualise our future, where our vision, our goals, have come true - and anchor ourselves to that point today, right here, right now.

Exercise: Define Your Vision

Note down your definition of what your vision - and your business - will look like for you in five years' time.

Now close your eyes, and visualise that success.

_____
_____
_____
_____

What does it look like? Feel like? Sound like?

_____
_____
_____
_____

Make That Vision Stick

Your vision spreads because of a reinforcing process of increased clarity, enthusiasm, communication and commitment. As people talk, the vision grows clearer. As it grows clearer, enthusiasm for its benefits builds.

There can be limiting factors that slow growth, such as a lack of faith in the future. Your vision only becomes a living force when people truly believe they can shape their future, thanks to your vision.

An unwavering belief in your vision is what motivates you - and your team - to get up and go to work each day. If you lose faith, everything will begin to crumble.

Living in Parallel Universes: Now and Then

Of course, your unshakeable faith has to be tempered by actual reality - so do consider the facts!

When business author Jim Collins spoke with Admiral James Stockdale, who survived horrendous torture in the notorious 'Hanoi Hilton' for seven years during the Vietnam war, Colllins asked the hero about his coping strategy during his time in the Vietnamese POW camp. When Collins asked which prisoners didn't make it, Stockdale replied:

"Oh, that's easy, the optimists. They were the ones who said, 'We're going to be out by Christmas.' And Christmas would come, and Christmas would go. Then they'd say, 'We're going to be out by Easter.' And Easter would come, and Easter would go. And then Thanksgiving, and then it would be Christmas again. And they died of a broken heart. This is a very important lesson.

> *You must never confuse faith that you will prevail in the end—which you can never afford to lose—with the discipline to confront the most brutal facts of your current reality, whatever they might be."*
> **- Admiral James Stockdale**

Collins labelled this harsh lesson the 'Stockdale Paradox'. What this translates to for the purposes of this chapter is that we have to learn how to accept the brutal facts of reality, while maintaining unwavering faith in the end game/vision - and that's the paradox.

We know life can be unfair – sometimes to our advantage, other times to our disadvantage – but acceptance of this teaches us how to deal with the inevitable difficulties in life.

Develop faith that you will prevail in the end, regardless of the difficulties, but do not shirk away from the facts.

You need to be able to embrace change, not resist or fear change, but totally embrace it.

But first, before you can change and grow, you need to understand what your starting point is, and what your own limits, your motivation and your emotional stakes are.

As well as letting go, discussed in the last chapter, you need to learn to accept failure.

Part of living in the future but being present now is acceptance that failure happens. I've stepped into many a corporate culture where there is a palpable fear of failure.

But think of failure as simply a way of growing, and of learning.

Look at people like Thomas Edison, or more recently, Dyson. They both failed a lot before hitting on their great idea - and they resolutely held onto their vision. James Dyson famously admitted he made "5,127 prototypes of my vacuum before I got it right. There were 5,126 failures. But I learned from each one. That's how I came up with a solution."

Image by Eva Rinaldi, CC BY-SA 2.0, via Wikimedia Commons

Today, Dyson is a billionaire, his vacuums are a market leader, and he says that it was failure and frustration that drove him on - he never lost sight of his vision.

Perseverance is also key - just look at the incredible story of Admiral James Stockdale, above. You've got to persevere, you may not get the results you want initially, but you need to treat obstacles as challenges and persist despite difficult situations, which allow you to go and move forward.

Have Faith Like Carrey

*Image by Ian Smith from London, England,
CC BY-SA 2.0, via Wikimedia Commons*

Hollywood 'A' list Actor Jim Carrey famously wrote himself a cheque for US$10million, for acting services, dated ten years in future. He had faith that one day, an acting role, or his career, would produce that kind of money.

He suffered rejection, and tough times. He did what he had to do to survive, yet he never lost faith that one day, he would become a successful film star.

And ten years after writing it, the now dog-eared cheque could be cashed: he secured $10m for his role in 'Dumb and Dumber'.

We all need to set our 'North Star' - that shining point in future - which might seem difficult to reach. The journey might be difficult, with unforeseen challenges and opportunities, but set your faith, set your vision and go for it!

The key point here is that if you set your sights on a goal that is easily achievable or imaginable, you haven't set a goal that's aspirational - and inspirational - enough. If you know exactly how you're going to get there, you haven't set the goal big enough for you or your team.

While we remain firmly rooted in the now, we must all keep an eye on that elusive future goal and vision.

Coaching questions

What problems are you facing today?

What plans have you in place to address your current challenges?

What don't you see?

What is your personal vision for success in five years' time?

Is your business vision aligned with this?

How do you connect with your personal and business vision on a daily basis?

CHAPTER 10

Strategy Five: Develop a Growth Mindset

"In [the growth] mindset, the hand you're dealt is just the starting point for development. Everyone can change and grow through application and experience."
-Carol Dweck, Mindset

"Live as if you were to die tomorrow; learn as if you were to live forever."
-Mahatma Gandhi

"Most of the important things in the world have been accomplished by people who have kept on trying when there seemed no hope at all."
-Dale Carnegie

"Work hard now. Don't wait. If you work hard enough, you'll be given what you deserve."
-Shaquille O'Neal

You Need to Grow Faster Than Your Company

That's in capital letters at the beginning of this chapter because it's such an important, yet basic, point to make, and yet, so many of us forget it.

If you're not driving the business, if you're not constantly looking for new knowledge, new ways of doing things, keeping up with the competition and industry trends, you'll simply stagnate.

And we're not about that.

A scale-up leader needs a certain kind of mindset.

And if you don't have that mindset, then this chapter is here to help you understand how to begin to develop it.

Fundamentally, there are two types of mindset - a **fixed mindset**, which is a firm belief system, created from the day you were born. Those with a fixed mindset don't believe they've got any particular sort of talent, but are simply born with innate abilities, or a lack of certain abilities. Their potential, in all areas of life, tends to be fixed and they don't believe it can be changed or adapted.

Fixed mindset people might be familiar to you - by the words they use, like "That's the hand I've been dealt" or "I'm not good at that" or" I can't do that". One of the worst phrases I've heard is: "I'll never be able to become that!" They have limited their potential simply by what they know of themselves, without making any allowances or opportunity for improvement.

Then you've got people with a **growth mindset**, which is a very different belief system. These are the people who recognise they've got abilities that they can hone, add to or develop throughout life. They believe they've got unlimited potential.

A growth mindset encourages positivity and forward-thinking. It embraces every wrong turn as a learning opportunity, not as a failure. A growth mindset provides an open-minded perspective that encourages improvement, which, in turn, leads to success.

Which mindset you have obviously dictates how you approach challenges. And as I'm sure you already realise, a fixed mindset won't get you far in the scale-up leadership journey.

Especially as we slowly extricate ourselves from the effects of the pandemic (*writing in Autumn 2021*), there's never been a better time to foster a growth mindset.

	Fixed Mindset	**Growth Mindset**
What they believe..	Intelligence is static	Intelligence can be developed "
How they behave...	Avoid challenges Give up easily See effort as fruitless Ignore useful negative feedback Feel threatened by the success of others	Embrace challenges Persist in the face of setbacks See effort as the path of mastery Learn from criticism Find inspiration from the success of others
What they get...	Plateau early and achieve less than full potential	Reach higher levels of achievement

Professionals who adopt a growth mindset put in the extra time and effort to understand why they failed, and rebound from setbacks quickly. Those with fixed mindsets believe their successes and failures are inextricably tied to their personal identities.

The key to higher achievement via the growth mindset lies in focusing on process more than ability, and has quantifiable results for achievement.

Keep a *fixed* mindset, and you're actually sabotaging your own success.

Microsoft's magnificent mindset

*Image by Brian Smale and Microsoft,
CC BY-SA 4.0, via Wikimedia Commons*

Microsoft is one of the only companies which has managed to maintain its position as one of the top five companies in the world by market capitalization. Its success is down to its growth mindset as a company - with a relentless focus on growth. When new CEO Satya Nadella took over the reins in 2014, he was focused on a growth mindset.

"You need new ideas and you need new capabilities, but the only way you're going to get those new ideas and new capabilities is if you have a culture that allows you to grow those."

Satya Nadella

He attributes the company turnaround that he spearheaded, at least in part, to Stanford psychologist Carol Dweck's book Mindset as inspiration for the company's culture change.

In her book, Dweck underscores the value of developing a growth mindset. Calling upon decades of research, she reveals that individuals who believe their talents can be developed through hard work, good strategies, and input from others (*i.e., a growth mindset*) tend to achieve more than those who believe their talents are innate gifts with finite development potential (*i.e., a fixed mindset*).

Nadella was insistent about instilling a growth mindset philosophy into Microsoft. A key part of this was defining what a Microsoft manager needs to be: someone with the ability to deliver success through empowerment, accountability, by modelling, coaching and caring.

They need to analyse a situation, and to learn from it, with a framework to assess what went well, learn from that and move forward.

This process is what helped make Microsoft relevant again.

There are those who might look at a situation and simply say "Well, I can't do anything about this, I've learned what I can, let's just move on."

But adopt a growth mindset, and you're more likely to fully analyse every situation as a positive learning experience, from which we can improve and make things work better next time.

A growth mindset means you're exposing yourself more to your inadequacies and your deficiencies, but using that exposure to learn, to develop and grow. Someone with a fixed mindset will simply think 'that's who I am' and carry on doing what they've always done.

A growth mindset is a positive one. Be willing to learn, to adapt, and to grow. Failure is just another tool in your growth arsenal.

Exercise: Do you Have a Fixed or Growth Mindset?

Take the following quiz to determine whether you have a mixed or growth mindset.

1. Circle the number for each question which best describes you

2. Total and record your score when you have completed each of the 10 questions

3. Use the score to determine your mindset

	Strongly Agree	**Agree**	**Disagree**	**Strongly Disagree**
Intelligence is something very basic about you that you can't change very much	0	1	2	3
No matter how much intelligence you have, you can change it quite a bit	3	2	1	0
Few people will be truly good at sports, you have to be born with the ability	0	1	2	3
The harder you work at something, the better you get	3	2	1	0
I often get angry when I get feedback about my performance	0	1	2	3
I appreciate when people, parents, coaches or teachers give me feedback about my performance	3	2	1	0
Truly smart people do not need to try hard	0	1	2	3
You can always change how intelligent you are	3	2	1	0
You are a certain kind of person and not much can be done to change that	0	1	2	3
I enjoy learning new things	3	2	1	0

Score Total

21-30 =   Strong growth mindset

16-20 =   Growth with some fixed ideas

11-15 =   Fixed with some growth ideas

0-10 =   Strong fixed mindset

Sponges and Rocks

Image by [Doha Stadium Plus Qatar from Doha, Qatar](#), [CC BY 2.0](#), via Wikimedia Commons

I was lucky enough to meet England's 2003 Rugby World Cup-winning coach Sir Clive Woodward, who talked about how he chose members of the winning squad.

> *"The way I leveraged talent is by categorising every player as either a sponge or a rock. Great teams make great individuals but the secret of their work is you need every individual in your team to have a sponge between their ears and a thirst for knowledge. If you have a rock in your team, the chance of beating someone with more talent than you is greatly reduced."*
> **- Sir Clive Woodward**

The coach gave players laptops, and installed cameras in the training stadium. This was the first time data analysis of player performance had been used in rugby. Players were given data on how they performed, and the chance to learn from it. Those who showed they learned from the new program - and adapted their game - were given the chance to trial for the squad, having demonstrated that they were 'sponges' - those able and willing to learn, to absorb new information, like a sponge. Those who didn't learn - the rocks - were excluded from the squad. New information bounces off a 'rock', and they are less agile.

Sir Clive is now a business coach, but during his time with the England squad he invited a wide range of successful business people to sit in on discussions with his England squad.

He then invited them to offer one idea or suggestion of how to do things better – and he ended up with 50 ideas, which he says help him to constantly improve.

How do you test if new recruits are a sponge or a rock? You need people on your team who are sponges, to step in and step up, displaying the ability to learn and adapt faster than your competitors. If you have a team committed to learning and moving forward with a growth mindset, part of the growth mindset is being open to learning, to new ideas, and to be a 'sponge' to information. They are open to new ideas, learning from situations and acting on that (new) information. This means they improve themselves, the team and business processes.

Companies which are going to succeed are those which are able to adapt to the environment they are playing in - or they're learning faster than their competitors.

And the only way you can do that is through learning.

Consider some of the most successful companies out there - the likes of Spotify, for example. Senior management at Spotify has to re-apply for their roles every year - because every role changes. Recognising this, Spotify keeps management on its toes, underlines the need to keep learning, and ensures the senior team remains relevant. They consider if their directors have the skills, the training, the commitment *and* the ability to learn and move to the next level.

This is a great way to ensure your company is always growing, with a growth mindset instilled from the top down.

A fixed mindset can kill dreams, ambition and certainly stymies growth. If you've got a company which isn't learning, which operates under a fixed mindset, I guarantee you won't be in business for too long.

Make yourself ready to drive change — whether yourself, your team, the organisational structure, or even your business direction and vision.

> *"The day the learn-it-all says, 'I'm done' is when you become a know-it-all. And so, to understand that paradox and to be able to confront your fixed mindset each day is that continuous process of renewal."*
> - Satya Nadella

How to Develop a Growth Mindset

Embrace change: The most effective modern leaders embrace the fact that we live in a rapidly changing world, and so must you. Don't fear it.

Develop self-awareness in terms of how you approach new situations. How do you approach change? Do you embrace change? Or resist it?

Understand yourself: Before you can change and grow, you need to understand what your starting point is, and what your own limits, motivations, and your emotional stakes are.

Always be learning: The Satya Nadella quote explains it all - once you stop learning, the growth mindset fades. To maintain a growth mindset, you shouldn't consider yourself an expert. If you do, learning stops.

Learn from the past, but keep focused on the future: Don't keep doing what you've always done....and use a growth mindset to keep learning how to achieve your goals and strive towards your vision.

Disrupt Yourself: The coolest element here, in my humble opinion, is we should all learn to disrupt ourselves. The theory goes, according to Mark Sanborn, author of The Potential Principle, that leaders need to disrupt themselves before something else does it for them. If change like a disruptive technology comes from somewhere else, you might struggle to adapt. But if you drive innovation, that makes _you_ the game-changer!

Develop the Right Habits for a Growth Mindset

- Define your learning outcomes
- Have a plan – ask what you want to learn
- Identify your preferred modes of learning – E.g., reading, podcasts, watching videos, or experiential learning, for example
- Build a learning habit - Every day...see The *Miracle Morning*
- FOCUS – Follow One Course Until Successful - don't try and learn everything!
- Integrate learning – Put what you've learned into practice as soon as possible, or teach your newly-acquired knowledge to somebody else.

Practice What You Preach

In 2016, Microsoft launched a frontier-breaking Twitter bot named Tay. The aim of the experiment was to understand - and advance - how artificial intelligence might communicate with real people in real time.

Just 16 hours after launch, Tay was shut down, after hackers manipulated the account to spew racism and profanity. After issuing an official apology, CEO Nadella sent an email to the team behind the tumultuous Tay: "Keep pushing, and know that I am with you," Nadella wrote. "[The] key is to keep learning and improving."

Coaching Questions

Are there areas in your life or business where your mindset is fixed?

What practices do you have that help build a growth mindset on a daily basis?

Recognising your team is a reflection of yourself - how well does your team reflect a growth mindset?

What else can you do to encourage a learning mentality within your business?

CHAPTER 11

Strategy Six: Be a Clockbuilder

> *"The great use of life is to spend it for something that will outlast it."*
> **-William James**

> *"Please think about your legacy because you are writing it every day."*
> **-Gary Vaynerchuk**

When you have a single great idea, or when you are considered to be a charismatic, visionary leader, this is known as "time telling". But building a company that succeeds beyond the influence of any single leader - and through multiple product life cycles is called "clock building."

Time telling is an instant act; something that is impermanent, fleeting and forgettable. Clock building is creating something solid, reliable, memorable and built to last.

Meanwhile, renowned US business management author and consultant, Jim Collins' research deflated two widely-held myths in business teaching: the myth of the great idea and of the great and charismatic leader.

In his book '<u>Good to Great</u>' - one of the best-selling management books of all time - Collins posited that creating and building a visionary company does not require either a great idea - or a great leader. Furthermore, Collins says there was evidence that great ideas from charismatic leaders might actually be negatively correlated with building a visionary company.

An American Ideal

In the 1700s, a country's greatness was seen to be dependent on how good its monarch was - a good king or queen guided the country towards the right path, or in the best interests of all.

But when what we know as the modern nation of America was founded, the leaders joined together to build an enduring constitution; a set of rules to abide by which went beyond one person, one charismatic leader.

The leaders didn't ask "Who should be president?" but rather focused on asking "What processes can we create that will give us good presidents long after we're dead and gone? What type of enduring country do we want to build? What guidelines and mechanisms should we construct that will give us the kind of country we envision?"

As Collins puts it, Thomas Jefferson, James Madison, and John Adams were not charismatic visionary leaders - but they were organisational visionaries.

They were clock builders.

Clock building, then, is about creating an enduring company that will survive beyond your leadership. If your company is completely reliant on you, clearly, its growth will be limited.

As a scale-up leader, you must lead by example, you must ensure your vision is held steady, and you must get everyone on the bus heading in the right direction and knowing the destination. But if you are a 'time teller', you are simply focused on your own 'genius', rather than building a company culture that is the genius. The company takes on a life of its own, backed, supported and driven by you and your management team, but not wholly reliant on you.

The strategy here is to think beyond your own leadership, your own vision. A visionary company focuses on making the company durable. The company should be bigger than you, and can actually help make you a better business leader.

Time-Tellers vs Clock Builders

Time Tellers:

Are small thinkers	Focus on the minutia	Think mostly about themselves
Keep information to themselves	Hoard their gifts	Exclude others
Are 'all-knowing'	Make themselves indispensable	Are ego focused
Take all the credit	Are present-oriented	

Clock Builders:

Are visionaries	See the big picture	Think most about others and the greater good
Share information freely	Give their gifts away in service to others	Are legacy-oriented
Accept and include others	Acknowledge they don't know it all	Understand the potential of their team
Make others indispensable	Share the credit with others	Are humble

Shoot for Level Five Leadership

Collins also identified five levels of leadership. At Level One are highly capable individuals. At this level, your work makes great contributions, you use all your skills and knowledge, and have the talent to do a good job.

Level Two leaders are known as contributing team members. These leaders use knowledge and skills to help the team succeed, and work effectively, productively and successfully with other people. At Level Three, we have competent managers. These leaders are able to organise groups effectively to achieve specific goals and objectives.

Level Four leaders are described as effective leaders – and this is where most leaders are categorised. You are able to galvanise a department, team or an entire business to meet performance objectives and achieve your vision.

But Level Five leaders recognise it is not about them. They are simply stewards, there to serve a cause. They recognise it is more important to get the right people on the bus versus where the bus is going. They are humble. They walk a tightrope between personal humility and professional will. Characterised by respect for people, their unselfish perspective, and by a relentless focus on results, Level Five people are simply great leaders.

BE A LEVEL 5 LEADER

5. Great Leader
4. Effective Leader
3. Competent Manager
2. Contributing Team Member
1. Highly Capable Individual

Source: Good to Great, Jim Collins

Exercise: What Level Are You At?

Take a moment here to think about people you've worked with, heard speak, or read about. Who fits the Level Five leader description?

_____
_____
_____

Whose leadership style do you most admire, and who would you most like to emulate?

_____
_____
_____

Ask yourself how your leadership legacy will impact people in future.

_____
_____
_____

We can talk about Steve Jobs, Bill Gates and Elon Musk as Level Five leaders, but there are other inspirational, Level Five leaders in a number of much smaller, scale-up companies - go look for a mentor, an inspirational leader, someone with the values you aspire to, in your local network.

Of course, one of the interesting things about Level Five leaders is that you might not have heard of many of them (check out former Kimberly-Clark CEO Darwin Smith, here) - that's part of the territory - they're not in it for personal recognition, for ego - they're too busy building a great company.

Assess your own situation.

> *"Are you driven more by your fears – of not being able to pay your bills, of losing your job, of failing? Or are you driven by the knowledge that you, like every one of us, have the capacity to do amazing things?"*
> **-Trevor Wilson, CEO of TWI Inc.**

Business leaders striving to create something that will leave the world a better place are not only more engaged themselves, but they're more likely to take actions that help their employees engage. While leaders at the other four levels can produce high degrees of success, it's not enough to drive companies from mediocrity to sustained excellence. For that, you need to aim for Level Five leadership.

Level 5 Leadership Hacks

OK, that title might be 'clickbait' - there is no easy, quick way to become a Level Five leader. And if you're looking for 'hacks' to get there, you're in the wrong game. To become a great leader, you must simply build your skills - and the ten skills we highlight in this book are a start.

Truly great leaders tend to display a specific blend of skills. But they also possess something else - a certain set of characteristics which are hard to define.

And it seems somewhat counterintuitive to conventional wisdom - we expect great companies to be led by 'larger than life' characters, right? But Level Five leaders tend to be disciplined, humble and passionate. They don't desire the limelight, or to be revered. And interestingly, Collins suggests that while they show humility, they also have the skills to lead with iron will, and drive the business forward with great strength of character.

In striving to become a Level Five leader, you should have already mastered the skills on the lower rungs. By virtue of reading this book, you've already shown you have a desire for learning, and for development.

But key to Level Five leadership is a sense of humility. Try to learn to be (more) humble, and understand why arrogance is destructive. A first step might be to remember to credit teams and key team members for hard work - while accepting responsibility for team efforts when things go wrong.

Discipline is also key - taking a strong, disciplined stance to your work is leading by example, as is sticking to your guns - while respectfully taking on board other's opinions.

On the other hand, always being willing to ask for help - while admitting your weaknesses and strengths - is another Level five trait. Calling on the expertise of others is another sign of humility and of a clock-building attitude.

Like every good leader, a top Level five leader will surround themselves with the best talent they can find (and perhaps afford) - and help them reach their full potential. Being passionate - and sharing that passion - is also part of the journey to Level Five leadership. Showing you love the company and what you do will surely inspire others. Working with purpose is a sure-fire way to leap out of bed in the morning full of positive energy!

A Level Five leader has 'let go' of the assumptions, the characteristics and the beliefs which are holding them, and the company back. Are you ready to 'let go' and be a clock builder?

Coaching questions

Are you time telling or clock building?

What legacy would you like your business to leave behind?

Is your leadership team clock building?

Are you a level 3, 4 or 5 leader?

Would your team call you a level 3, 4 or 5 leader?

How do you become a level 5 leader? What must change?

CHAPTER 12

Strategy Seven: Become a Multiplier

> *"Concentrate on measuring performance and winning will take care of itself. That is a brilliant excuse for coming second."*
> **-Clive Woodward**

> *"Anything that is measured and watched, improves."*
> **-Bob Parsons**

> *"If your actions inspire others to dream more, learn more, do more and become more, you are a leader."*
> **-John Quincy Adams**

> *"Leaders instil in their people a hope for success and a belief in themselves. Positive leaders empower people to accomplish their goals."*
> **-Unknown**

Gladstone and Disraeli

In 2009, on a flight back from the US, I picked up Time Magazine. In it, there was an article about the Top 100 Most Influential People. I came across this quote from Jennie Jerome, Winston Churchill's mother, responding to a journalist who asked her what she thought after meeting two potential British Prime Ministers: "When I left the dining room after sitting next to Gladstone, I thought he was the cleverest man in England. But when I sat next to Disraeli, I left feeling that I was the cleverest woman."

William Gladstone and his rival Benjamin Disraeli had very different personalities. Disraeli apparently spent the evening asking her questions and listening intently to her responses.

But Disraeli - the person who had mastered the art of making other people feel important - went on to win the election.

Disraeli's differentiating factor was that he had (naturally) mastered the art of making other people feel brilliant, respected, and important — a key secret of charismatic leaders.

While Disraeli was clearly a Multiplier, the undoubtedly brilliant Gladstone was obviously a Diminisher.

During the rest of that flight, I thought about all those managers and leaders I had worked for which made me feel great – the smartest person in the room (the Disraelis) compared to those who demotivated me – those who believed they were the smartest person in the room (the Gladstones).

Exercise: Which Leaders Have Affected Your Own Leadership Style?

Who was a diminisher to you? How did they behave?

_____

_____

Who was a multiplier to you? And how did they behave?

_____

_____

In her fantastic book '*Multipliers*' the renowned leadership coach Liz Wiseman identifies two types of leaders - Diminishers and Multipliers.

Diminishers consider *themselves* to be geniuses, while Multipliers are genius *makers*.

A leader 'diminishes' by their belief that people have scarce intelligence. They believe people won't figure things out themselves unless they are there to dictate what must be done. They think themselves invaluable and irreplaceable.

Diminishers tend to 'empire build' and underutilise talent. They create anxiety and suppress thinking, preferring to tell their people what to do - and they make decisions in isolation. Diminishers micromanage, take over and wield control akin to dictators - it's literally "their way or the highway."

The five disciplines of Multipliers:

- Attract and optimise talent
- Require peoples best thinking
- Extend challenges

- Debate decisions
- Instil accountability

The five traits of Diminishers

- Empire builders
- Tyrants
- 'Know it alls'
- Take all the decisions
- Micromanage

Multipliers, on the other hand, see the innate intelligence in all of us, and strive to help people work things out for themselves, trusting in their team's natural ability.

Multipliers attract the best talent, by encouraging autonomy and personal problem solving. They empower their people to take ownership of challenges, encouraging problem-solving, debate and decision-making. They allow people to have ownership of specific departments, roles or tasks, with accountability. A Multiplier allows learning, and is humble enough to always look to learn from their talent.

As you might envisage, a work culture led by a Diminisher sees people only giving 50% of what they are truly capable of. In other words, where you work for a Diminisher, you're going to do just enough to get by. You'll probably experience resentment when asked to do more for a Diminisher, especially if that extra work leads to failure. Clearly, these environments are unfulfilling, unrewarding and pretty miserable workplaces!

Multipliers inspire individuals to go and do stuff for them, understanding what their work will lead to, feeling supported and empowered. Multipliers mostly get 100% effort from their teams - so you're effectively doubling what a person is capable of - doubling your workforce for free, simply by backing them in their role in a positive, supportive way.

Multipliers are leaders who create more leaders, not more followers.

Diminishers bring out the worst in people.

	Diminisher	Multiplier
What they believe..	Scarce Intelligence in the Team People won't figure it out without me"	Abundant Intelligence in the Team "People are smart and will figure it out"
How they behave...	Builder Empires Horde and underutilize talent Tyranical Create anxiety and suppress thinking Know-It-Alls Tell people what to do Make Decisions Make isolated decisions Micromanage Take over and control	Attract Talent Attract and optimise talent Liberate Create intensity that requires best thinking Challenge Extend challenges Encourage Debate Debate before deciding Invest Instill ownership and accountability

Let's be honest here. As a coach, I have worked with many leaders who, as they move from start-up to scale-up, many of us will have unwittingly adopted a 'Diminisher' style of leadership. Creating a business often comes from *your* vision, and *your* goals. You hire people and expect everyone to align with your goals. In the entrepreneurial phase, you've proven your business model, you've got a business that works, and you *need* to be a Diminisher, simply because you're doing everything, you're controlling everything, you're setting up processes and making all the decisions in isolation.

But as your company grows, so must your management style. You must let go of your old dictatorial management style - and lean in to the joys of becoming a Multiplier and the associated freedom that brings. This means changing your habits and who you have been as a leader, before metamorphosing into a new version of yourself.

And where there is pressure to make a decision, there's always the danger of becoming an accidental diminisher. You tell people what's going to happen, and make a decision solo. You accidentally slip back into micromanaging the team. This is obviously detrimental to your staff, who are left undermined and feeling untrusted. We all want to be a Multiplier, but our management style sits somewhere on the bell curve, below, and can be quite fluid.

BEWARE THE ACCIDENTAL DIMINISHER

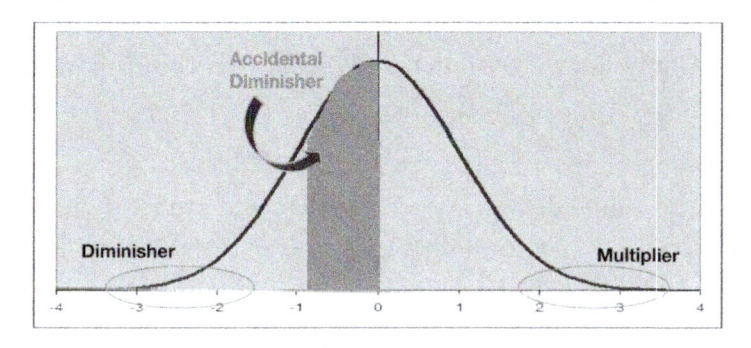

Leadership starts with honing your self-awareness. If you're aware of yourself and how your leadership style impacts others, that's going to increase your awareness of others, which in turn enables you to increase your Emotional Intelligence (EQ) score and have a more positive impact.

This is perhaps best explained in a chart:

ALL CHANGE STARTS WITH SELF AWARENESS

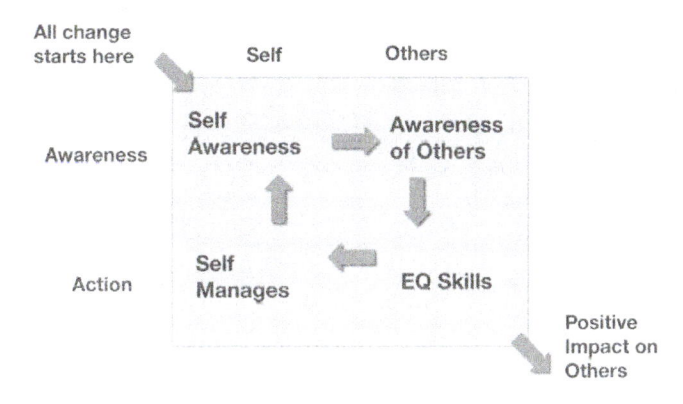

Unfortunately, some of us simply don't have it in us to become a Multiplier. Some of us are set in our ways. In my experience, the path to becoming a Multiplier is only found through real world experience, coupled with a willingness to develop self-awareness and humility.

Rule your company with a Diminisher approach, and the 'A' players you attract to your team - based on your great concept and great plans, for

The Scale-Up Leader | 145

example, begin to lose confidence as you undermine and override their decisions. They stagnate, and stay with your company, feeling inadequate to move into another role elsewhere. So, this cycle of decline continues, and your 'A' team becomes very much a 'B' team, your company suffers and new talent won't be 'A' players either.

Take a Multiplier approach, and you'll attract 'A' Players, who will be given the chance to shine, deliver fantastic results, and attract more 'A' level talent. This cycle of attraction then leads to even better results, and a great company reputation with A+ staff.

Clearly, Wiseman hit on a fundamental point here - that your management style affects your company reputation and the bottom line!

How do you:	Diminisher	Multiplier
Manage talent?	Use	Develop
Approach mistakes?	Blame	Explore
Set direction?	Tell	Challenge
Make decisions?	Decide	Consult
Get things done	Control	Support

From Diminishing to Multiplying

The first steps to shift your management style are rooted in some simple soul-searching.

Ask your team how they feel you are performing as a leader, then think about how you can improve. Be thick-skinned, though - the answers might not be what you want to hear!

As with the higher leadership styles and levels we've discussed already, humility is a good trait to develop, as is transparency and perhaps a touch of vulnerability. Showing your passion is always a good idea.

Hearing from your team how they think you are doing is best approached from an open, positive mindset. Think of lessons you can take from the feedback, and what actions might be explored as a result of the feedback to up your game.

Coaching Questions

Is your leadership style more towards diminisher or multiplier?

Would your team describe you more as a multiplier or a diminisher?

What must you change to become more of a multiplier?

What must you let go to become more of a multiplier? Think about your habits, beliefs, need for control, for example?

CHAPTER 13

Strategy Eight: Think Slow

> *"Clear thinking requires courage rather than intelligence."*
> **-Thomas Szasz**

> *"Did you ever stop to think, and forget to start again?"*
> **-Winnie the Pooh**

> *"Few minds wear out; more rust out."*
> **-Christian N. Bovee**

Think slow? Doesn't that sound counterintuitive to the characteristics you need as a scale-up leader? Especially in today's super-fast-paced business environment.

But no, that's not the case. What we mean by 'think slow' really is a positive trait to develop.

As author and CEO Tony Schwartz puts it: "Speed is the enemy of nearly everything in life that really matters. It's addictive, and it undermines quality, compassion, depth, creativity, appreciation and real relationships."

Think slow: A Lesson in Judging a Situation

A farmer once had a horse run away. His neighbours were quite sympathetic, saying: "How awful for you."

He replied, "We'll see."

His son went to find the horse and came back triumphantly riding it. The neighbours exclaimed, "What joy; your horse has been found!" The farmer calmly said: "We'll see."

The farmer's son tried to break and train the temperamental horse, but was thrown from the horse and broke his leg. It required setting and binding and he could not work on his father's farm. The neighbours sadly pronounced: "How unfortunate for you! You will not have your son's help around the farm for several weeks. What a catastrophe!"

The farmer replied: "We'll see."

But one neighbour retorted, "How can you be so flippant about your son's predicament? I know you will have to work late into the night to get everything done. You may be in denial, but you DO have a serious problem!"

The farmer quietly said: "We'll see."

The following day, the Emperor's guard arrived to conscript all eligible men to fight a war. Because of his broken leg, the farmer's son was not carried off by the army. Because his horse was too unsettled, it was not conscripted. And because he had no horse or son to help him feed the rest of his family, he was left alone to tend to his farm.

This Taoist parable is interpreted in many ways, but for me, and for the purposes of teaching scale-up leadership skills, the biggest takeaway is that no event can really be judged as good or bad, lucky or unlucky, fortunate or unfortunate. Only time can tell the whole story, so think slow.

Getting some space between the story and reality might reduce stress and help us move through life more gracefully.

Donald Knuth, renowned mathematician and recipient of the ACM Turing Award (considered the Nobel Prize of computer science), stopped using email conventionally in 1990.

He issued a statement on his Stanford faculty page: "I have been a happy man ever since January 1, 1990, when I no longer had an email address. I'd used email since about 1975, and it seems to me that 15 years of email is plenty for one lifetime. Email is a wonderful thing for people whose role in life is to be on top of things. But not for me; my role is to be on the bottom of things. What I do takes long hours of studying and uninterruptible concentration."

Today, the computer scientist, a professor emeritus at Stanford University, uses a secretary to filter his email, and only checks his actual email inbox once every three months.

And what Knuth realised, and committed to, is the value of cutting out unnecessary distractions, to help productivity, and to help get the job done.

Slowly Does It

In a blog, prolific author and leadership consultant Rich Litvin talks about overcoming the guilt of being inactive to allow yourself the time to think. Allowing yourself solo time - call it a mini-retreat if you like - often leads to unexpected answers to some of your biggest issues.

Slowing down - often, away from the office or your laptop - allows your mind to drift towards unexpected possibilities, solutions and innovations.

As Litvin says: "Success is a combination of real effort, ravenous curiosity, deep reflection and a ferocious protection of your time off."

Litvin proudly proclaims his 'laziness' - in terms of working smarter, not harder.

Back Away from Burnout

For sure, the last few years have been tough, tinged with tragedy and many business closures.

It's been too easy to throw ourselves into our businesses, thinking that the harder we work, the more our business is likely to survive. As I mentioned earlier, I've seen clients thinking they can actually work their way out of the pandemic economic collapse - and they've ended up working even harder than they were previously, simply to try to survive, and try to move forward.

But that's not true - and for one overarching reason - burnout. A lack of focus, concentration and sleep, combined with stress leads to bad decision making, often rushed, and without consulting your team. You're so busy running things, fighting fire and solving urgent issues, there's never time to strategise, to plan, to look at the bigger picture.

> *"If you look at all the really important breakthroughs made in any field, what you will find is that the unplanned, unintended or fortuitous connection plays just as great a role as the planned, the processed and the organised."*
> **-Rory Sutherland, Ogilvy Group UK**

We all need to put the brakes on, and get off the hamster wheel. It's only a matter of time before exhaustion kicks in, and you get burned out. You've got to learn to take time out, and start making proper decisions which make your life easier.

Overwork, of course, leads to poor health, and poor health will inevitably mean you can no longer continue on your path to scale-up leadership. Put your health, family and thinking time ahead of everything else. Easier said than done?

There're some tips coming right up.

> *"I just sit in my office and read all day."*
> **Warren Buffet**

Investment guru Warren Buffet says he spends 80% of his work day reading. Bill Gates heads off to a remote log cabin for at least a couple of weeks a year, just to read and think, free from distraction.

I spend at least 30 minutes every day reading, and then thinking about what I've read, and how I can apply it to my own life.

Be More Cunning, Like Cunningham

On a cross-country flight across the US some years ago, I found myself sitting next to serial entrepreneur, speaker and author, Keith Cunningham - (widely held to be the 'Dad' in the best-selling book "*Rich Dad, Poor Dad*" by Robert T. Kiyosaki). I know I touched on this fortuitous meeting in Chapter 7, but it's worth re-visiting here.

Cunningham told me how he built 'think time' into his weekly planner. He said that despite a busy schedule, for a few hours every Friday, he allows himself to focus on the business and what's driving him.

What's more, he explained his lifetime commitment to learning.

He said in his life, he has never stopped growing, learning and refining his skills.

His philosophy is that to make the greatest impact, he knows he must first work on himself.

He admitted to being a prolific reader - books, newspapers and magazines.

He said he attends numerous seminars throughout the year, and researches new businesses and ideas. On top of his weekly 'think time', he allows himself to have a 'learning day' several times each month.

For a scale-up leader, caught up in the chaos and challenges of the day - this think time is essential. It's when those big ideas form; when you're going to get insights, in the time you give yourself to disengage from the day to day, from other people's agendas.

You might compare scaling a company to building a plane - while that plane is flying. Unless you allow yourself 'think time', in this case, how to make the plane stronger or faster, for example, you simply won't be able to keep the plane in the air.

Ring fence a regular time, with alarms if necessary, and anchor yourself in a quiet, comfortable spot. It's a good idea to have a notepad and pen to hand. Focus on one question at a time. This allows you to give the question the energy it deserves. The better the question, the more robust the answers. After factoring these sessions into your schedule, you'll find you become more adept at utilising more brain power to solve the questions of the day.

And while ideas that come out of these sessions are all well and good; they are worthless without execution. Have the conviction to follow up on your thoughts and ideas.

Top Tips for Slow Thinking

- Allow yourself a regimented regular time for thinking and reading
- Arm yourself with a notepad, pens or whatever you need to help you remember things, ask and resolve questions
- Start with a 45-minute block, once a week
- Focus on one question per thinking time. This allows you to give each question the energy it deserves. My questions are designed to help me think about a problem or situation where I am uncertain (or too certain), stuck, or have been unrealistic in my thinking, which is usually a sign that I am about to do something stupid!

- Find a quiet spot without any distractions. The local coffee shop is not a great place because it's unpredictable and full of distractions. Your normal desk isn't a great spot either. Choose a different environment.

- Set a 45-minute timer.

- Start writing. What you'll find is that the first several minutes will be easy. You'll get all the low hanging fruit answers out of the way. Towards the end you'll find that it takes serious brain muscle to get that last 20% out. Those final ideas are going to be your best ones.

- Execute them! Ideas are useless without execution.

Exercise: Your Problems and Answers

Write down your three biggest business problems (e.g., cash flow, sales, supply chain).

Your answers will tend to be things like 'we have no cash'. Thinking time will allow you the chance to explore all the obstacles to getting cash; or rather, the obstacles that lie between the actual problem and where you are.

What obstacles are preventing you from being where you want to be and achieving what you want to achieve?

In one sentence, we need to slow down to speed up. Factoring in some 'breathing space' into your busy life will only ever reap benefits.

Thinking slow will help you act faster.

Questions, Questions

Settle yourself in for your first 45 minutes of slow think time - and consider some of these:

- Who is your target market?
- What do they think is important?
- If you deliver it to them, will they buy?
- How is this different from your competitors?
- What internal processes must you excel at to deliver on this Value Success Proposition?
- Are your outcomes and compensation structure aligned with producing these processes so that you can deliver those outcomes?
- How big would your business be if you still had every customer who had ever tried you?
- What can you do to keep the customers you currently have?
- What should be getting done that is not getting done because you are doing the minor and not the major things?
- What should you be doing, that would add more value?
- What are you currently doing that could be done by someone else?
- What can you (and only you) do?
- If you only had someone on my team who could _____ , you could double the size of my business.
- If your future success is 100% dependent on the support of others, whose support do you need?
- Where are you hanging on to answers which were great answers in a different environment?
- Which part of your business needs to adapt to the realities of today's environment?

- What employees were wonderful 5-10 years ago, but are simply not up to the job today?
- Which strategies got you here but are no longer the difference that makes the difference? Where are you obsolete or irrelevant?
- What question do you need to ask?
- Where are you avoiding paying the price of hard work or learning and practising new skills? Where are you searching for shortcuts where none exist?
- What are the ordinary things that need to be done on a consistent basis which will produce the desired outcomes?
- Where are you letting perfect get in the way of possible?
- What are the strategies you need to explore or the skills you need to learn that are outside your comfort zone?
- What do you need to try that will be done poorly (at the beginning) but which is critical for your success?
- If you could devote 100% of your time to just one type of customer, who (specifically) would it be? What do they "look" like?
- What are the 5 biggest problems/pains/issues of your ideal customers? Where are they frustrated?
- What can you do for customers that no one else is doing?
- What skills would you need to acquire?
- What resources would you need to double my sales?
- Who is your ideal target customer? How do they define success? What success can you give them that differentiates you from the competition and can be delivered profitably? What internal processes must you excel at to deliver this success proposition? Who do we need on our team to deliver on this proposition?
- What are you practising? Are you improving?
- How do your customers, clients and target market define success... specifically? Where is the mismatch between what you currently

offer and what they really want? What must you change to give the customer certainty that if they buy it, they will get the desired result?

- What assumptions are you making, that you are not aware you are making, that gives you what you see? What if your thinking is wrong... then what might be true? Remember to ask yourself, "What DON'T you see?"

- Your competitive advantage is based on who is hustling the most...Who's getting it done...Who is hitting deadlines...Who is delighting customers...Who is executing, kicking the can and putting rubber on the road on the most consistent basis. Are you winning this competition? What have been some of my mistakes and what lessons did you learn?

- Where are you stuck? What is the question you need to develop to help you find a solution?

- What are you doing to inspire and lead your team?

Coaching questions

Where do you think best?

What is stopping you from building in think time on a weekly basis?

How can you turn the output from your think time into actions?

What great "strategies" have you hatched in the past from think time that are viable but not getting implemented?

CHAPTER 14

Strategy Nine: Be Unfuckwithable

> *"In order to truly be unfuckwithable, you need to lose your need to seek validation or love from others and to judge them when you perceive that they are not giving you what you need."*
> **-Vishen Lakhiani,** The Code of the Extraordinary Mind

> *"When you innovate, you've got to be prepared for people telling you that you are nuts."*
> **-Larry Ellison**

> *"Play by the rules, but be ferocious."*
> **-Phil Knight, founder, Nike**

> *"UNFUCKWITHABLE: When you're truly at peace and in touch with yourself. Nothing anyone says or does bothers you and no negativity can touch you."*
> **-Vishen Lakhiani**

Unfuckwithable? That's got your attention, right? Tony Robbins famously swears during his life-changing seminars to shock his audiences into paying (more) attention utilising what's known as "the science of taboo language." Here, it's simply because it's a great way of describing what you need to be!

Think about it. Elon Musk. Jeff Bezos. Richard Branson. They're unfuckwithable.

A scale-up leader shouldn't need to swear to make a point clearer, but there are always exceptions. For the rest of this chapter - and because it's a long word - we'll refer to 'unfuckwithable' as UNFW.

Of course, there are other words to describe the state of being UNFW. Think of it as being:

Unshakeable.

Resilient.

Confident.

Unbothered by the opinion of others.

Ambitious.

Fierce.

Happy in your skin.

Self-reliant.

Self-assured.

Unapologetically you.

Living the life you've always wanted - and it also means full engagement with being, becoming, and overcoming the best possible version of yourself.

And although these are all key elements - no word sums all these up so well as UNFUCKWITHABLE!

So how do you become UNFW? Based on my experience, the leaders that are most UNFW exhibit the following eight characteristics...

The Scale-Up Leader | 163

- They realise they are worthy
- They focus on what they can control
- They don't seek validation
- They practice radical forgiveness
- They are rule-breakers
- They live fearlessly
- They step out of their comfort zone
- They have the right end goals

These are explored in more detail later in this chapter.

Exercise: How Unfuckwithable Are You?

Note your score next to each characteristic, 1 being low, 5 being high.

Characteristic   **Score 1-5**

- Seeking validation
- Practising radical forgiveness
- Being a rule breaker
- Living fearlessly
- Stepping out of your comfort zone
- Having the right end goals

Score Total

Score over 24: Totally UNFW

Score between 20-24: On the way to becoming UNFW

Score between 15-19: Starting out as UNFW

Score between 9-14: Heading in an UNFW direction

Score under 8: Still need to get off the starting blocks

Realise You Are Worthy

Having the belief you are enough - for example, your expectation of being praised or noticed and thanked – is tough. We can't, and shouldn't, wait around for praise and validation from others. Avoid creating meaning around others' actions or judge others who don't provide what you need. The chances are that you are compensating for a 'hole' within yourself that they reminded you of. This boils down to one of the most basic human fears - the root cause - that you are not enough.

Do others think you're worthy? It doesn't matter!

Your self-worth is a strength that obliterates other people's doubts and insecurities regarding you. *"In fact, your self-worth is so robust that it is able to alchemize the negative energy vomited up from others and then transform it into positive reinforcement and personal motivation"* (see Gary Z McGee, [Seven Signs You May Be Unfuckwithable](#)). Your unfuckwithability is multi-edged.

This starts with an understanding of yourself – your values, emotions, and how you live your life. Understanding, and gaining, a strong sense of self-worth is perhaps the most vital tool in your journey to becoming UNFW.

Remember, your bank account, job title, attractiveness, and social media following have nothing to do with how valuable or worthy a person you are. Take the time to recognise what values you admire in judging someone else's worth - qualities like compassion, kindness, empathy, respect for others, and how well they treat those around them.

There are some great worksheets and tips here for improving your self-worth [here](#) - which is probably worth a chapter to itself, but too much to go into here. Suffice to say a sense of self-worth is a useful element in your scale-up leadership arsenal, but don't tie your entire self-worth to your work.

> *"Being unfuckwithable is having confident vulnerability in the face of a world playing at being invulnerable."*
> **Annette O'Toole**

Focus on What You Can Control, Let Go of What You Can't

You can't control how other people act, but you can control how *you* act. And you act with full acceptance of other people's freedom. Should their freedom not give you what you think you need, don't whine or complain about it, but try to live by healthy example.

Most of us externalise our perceived lack of success - or failures - on external things. We blame the economy, our family, our education, our lack of time or money...it's too easy to blame others when things don't work out the way we want. But we need to look inside ourselves to tap into unlimited success.

Jack Canfield's success formula puts you in control:

E + R = O (Events + Response = Outcome)

When we don't like an outcome, we tend to blame the event (E) for the lack of results (O).

Canfield says the deciding factor in success is not the external conditions and circumstances. It's how you choose to respond (R).

Successful people simply change their responses (R) to events (E) - until they get the outcomes (O) they want. They don't blame any external factors - on the basis that if we continue to blame external factors for lack of success, nobody would ever succeed. As Canfield says: "For every reason it's not possible, there are hundreds of people who have faced the same circumstances and succeeded."

Too often in life we feel like we're the victim of bad circumstances and we just throw our hands up in resignation, saying there's nothing we can do about it. That is a cop out, and you can't be UNFW if you're living in a victim mentality, period.

It's time to make an important distinction. Take a close look around every corner of your life. Everything will fall squarely into one of two categories: the things we can change, and the things we cannot. And if you're honest with yourself, the things in the 'Can Change' bucket are probably upwards of 90% of what you're considering.

Here's a nice summary:

```
                        Focus
                          |
         WASTING          |      GREAT
         ENERGY           |      STATE OF
                          |      MIND
                          |
Cannot Control ───────────┼─────────── Can Control
                          |
                          |      WASTING
         PARANOID         |      OPPORTUNITIES
                          |
                        Ignore
```

At any given stage in your life, regardless of the set of circumstances you are dealing with, you can find yourself in one of four mental states:

Quadrant #1: Wasting your energy. When you focus on what is not within your control, you're wasting energy on factors that will not move you forward. This is like having a vacation booked, which was cancelled due to the pandemic. You can complain all you want, but what's the use? Stop draining your energy on it and start thinking clearly.

Quadrant #2: Being paranoid. When you ignore what is not within your control, you're being paranoid. You shouldn't ignore external factors, instead, accept what is and be aware of the external conditions outside your control. For instance, with the pandemic, it's important we maintain an understanding of the situation and how it progresses because it impacts our lives. We don't want to give it our undivided attention, but we do want to stay educated on it.

Quadrant #3: Wasting opportunities. When you ignore what is within your control, you're flat-out wasting opportunities. You're being unreasonable. You cannot control the weather, the laws, the economy, but you *can* control your attitude, how you spend your time and who you choose to hang out with. Stop being wasteful - and start using your time wisely for creativity and productivity.

Quadrant #4: Great state of mind. Focus on what is within your control, and you're in the driver's seat. You're being intentional about your attitude and how you spend your energy. This is where you are being emotionally mature and thinking rationally and clearly in a sunshine state of mind. And what does it do to you? It keeps you positive, energised, and motivated.

The above is adapted from a blog by the writer and researcher Omar Itani. You can read more here.

> *"When you are truly genuine, there will invariably be people who do not accept you. And in that case, you must be your own badass self, without apology."*
> -Katie Goodman

Do Not Seek Validation

Like yourself as if your life depends upon it - because it does. It doesn't matter if everybody likes you or if everybody hates you. What matters is that you like yourself, and self-love begins with healthy living in mind, body, and soul.

You are UNFW because hatred and adoration alike slide off you, like water off a duck's back. Self-validation is a useful skill. And while we all seek validation - from the day we're born, we seek validation from our parents, from our family, our friends and wider society - it's a sign of being interdependent and relying on feedback and encouragement from others.

That's not being UNFW, right?

The unfuckwithable you does not put the opinion, approval, or recognition of someone else over your own feelings.

Scale-up leaders do not look for other people's approval. You've got complete confidence in yourself. I think one of the key mistakes a lot of people tend to focus on is comparing themselves to others, comparing themselves to other leaders.

As former US President Theodore Roosevelt famously said: "Comparison is the thief of joy," and even in the Bible there's several references to how we shouldn't compare ourselves to others, suggesting it's foolish to do so, and leads to sadness.

Of course, as soon as you start comparing yourself to others, you can't be yourself, you cannot be authentic. But you're on your own journey. It doesn't matter what anybody else thinks. Be yourself.

> *"A flower does not think of competing with the flower next to it. It just blooms."*
> **-Koshin Ogui**

Practice Radical Forgiveness

Be the duck. Stress, fear, anxiety - all water off your being-the-duck's back.

If you want to be at your best, you need to constantly come up with ideas and insights - basically work at the highest level of creativity. But if you're holding a grudge against somebody, if you haven't forgiven somebody, those grudges tend to create anger within you.

And anger suppresses alpha waves - brain waves associated with focus, compassion and love - and helping achieve a calm, meditative state. You need those alpha waves to keep the creative juices flowing.

Simply put, we need to learn to forgive people. When you let go of toxic grudges, there's nothing holding you back. You can achieve a state of mind attuned to developing creative insights and ideas to drive you forward - and that makes you unfuckwithable.

Two Monks and a Woman

A senior monk and a junior monk were travelling together. They came to a river with a strong current. As the monks were preparing to cross it, they saw a very young and beautiful woman also attempting to cross.

The young woman asked if they could help her cross to the other side.

The two monks glanced at one another because they had taken vows not to touch a woman.

Then, without a word, the older monk picked up the woman, carried her across the river, placed her gently on the other side, and carried on his journey.

The younger monk couldn't believe what had just happened. After rejoining his companion, he was speechless, and an hour passed without a word between them.

Two more hours passed, then three, finally the younger monk could contain himself any longer, and blurted out "As monks, we are not permitted to touch a woman, how could you then carry that woman on your shoulders?"

The older monk looked at him and replied, "Brother, I set her down on the other side of the river, why are you still carrying her?"

> *"Why do you stay in prison when the door is so wide open?"*
> **-Rumi**

Upset the apple cart

Image by Terra Slaybaugh on Unsplash

Rules. Love them or hate them, they are a big part of every aspect of all our lives. But we shouldn't be afraid to break them. If they are valid, logical and work towards the greater good, then we should probably work with them. But if not, go ahead and break 'em! Learn to live a courage-based lifestyle, rather than languishing, unfulfilled, in a comfort-based lifestyle.

Rule breakers are less likely to become rigid, complacent, or stagnant - and more able to reveal the rigidity, complacency and stagnation within others. And of course, in both history and business, the most memorable, innovative leaders form a proud list of dissenters.

If you break a rule and it turns out to be a bad decision, you're still gaining knowledge, and a lesson to learn from. Our mistakes help make us wise.

> *"Attitude is the difference between ordeal and adventure."*
> **-Karl Frei**

Live Fearlessly

When you're unfuckwithable, fear is fuel.

What scares us also serves to compel us.

You could lose everything or gain everything. Carl Jung said: "The difference between a good life and a bad life is how well you walk through the fire." You are UNFW because you must be prepared to burn yourself - and capable of burning others. In other words, you're not afraid of fear - or sometimes creating (a little healthy) fear in others.

Step Out of Your Comfort Zone

A comfort zone is a safe space, but greatness never comes from staying in a safe space. Look at every epic 'hero's journey' - there's always a challenge, often entering unknown territories or facing down your fears. Stepping out of your own comfort zone is one of the best ways to become unfuckwithable. Trying new things can be scary, but that's kind of the point.

So, on your journey to becoming UNFW, try to do one thing a day that scares you. Attempting to overcome one scary thing per day combines taking it gently, one step at a time, while learning to stretch yourself and step out of your comfort zone.

Have the Right End Goals

Tune into the right end goal - one that you have absolute control over, that none can take away from you, and that doesn't require leaning on others to achieve.

Make it a non-attachment goal – where happiness is not attached to the completion of your goals. Focus on how good it will feel when you achieve the goal.

Don't forget there are ***end goals*** and ***means goals***. Means goals define the many paths you can choose en route to the end goal.

Imagine you're desperate to attend a Tony Robbins seminar. This is an end goal, as it defines your desired outcome. You really want to be there and enjoy the experience, live and in-person. It's not a stepping stone to anything greater, and no substitute experience would produce the same result.

Now suppose a radio station is having a contest where the prize is a ticket for the seminar, and you want to win! That's a means goal. Winning the contest is not the final outcome you desire - It's just one of numerous ways that could lead to you attending the seminar.

But if you don't win the ticket (i.e. - fail at your means goal), you might still be able to achieve your end goal. You just need to pursue another way to get to the seminar.

End goals are best kept on one list, rarely changing, as part of your vision. Means goals can be kept on a separate, more dynamic list, and subject to change as situations, needs and desires evolve.

End goals tend to be specific, while means goals, while vaguer and more flexible, actually help bring more clarity and precision to achieving your end goals. A means goal can be shelved if it's not working, or become unattainable, in favour of another approach.

Take a moment to think about your ultimate end goals - in business and life. Now consider your current means goals - what you need to do to help you smooth the route to those end goals.

Coaching Questions

Who do you know who is UNFW? What lessons can you take from their actions and behaviours?

What must you *start* doing to become more UNFW?

What must you *stop* doing to become more UNFW?

What must you *continue* doing to become more UNFW?

CHAPTER 15

Strategy 10: Master your Tennis Game

> *"The single biggest problem in communication is the illusion that it has taken place."*
> **-George Bernard Shaw**

> *"Communication is a skill that you can learn. It's like riding a bicycle or typing. If you're willing to work at it, you can rapidly improve the quality of every part of your life."*
> **-Brian Tracy**

Tennis might sound like an odd segue in a book like this, but mastering your tennis game is simply a metaphor for good communication.

To enjoy a successful tennis game, players must respond to what the other person is doing on the court. You must always be hitting that ball!

A poor communicator is one who simply waits for the other person to finish speaking so they can continue with their own agenda.

A good communicator knows better. Scale-up leaders understand how to empathise with individuals, and have highly honed skills of persuasion. Better communicators will automatically accelerate growth - whether it's marketing your product, getting your vision out to your team, or understanding, empathising and motivating individuals on your team.

Your ability to communicate as a leader will determine how fast and effortlessly you grow. For example, unless you can communicate your vision effectively you will not engage your team, suppliers, and customers, for example – to help you where you want to go.

If you cannot communicate effectively, then you're setting yourself up to waste your precious time by repeating that message again and again. As a scale up leader, do you really have time for this? Your ability to communicate well - to persuade, negotiate and possibly overcome objections - will determine how fast you grow As your team grows, so do individual relationships and the complexity of communication (we've all heard of Chinese whispers - where a message can be lost due to misheard repetition).

Without Excellent Communication, Chaos Ensues

The number one thing great communicators have in common is a heightened sense of situational and contextual awareness. The best communicators are great listeners and astute in their observations.

Great communicators are skilled at reading a person or group by sensing the moods, dynamics, attitudes, values and concerns of those being communicated with. Not only do they read their environment well, but they possess the ability to adapt their messaging to that environment without missing a beat.

The message is not about the messenger, it is 100% about meeting the needs and expectations of those you're communicating with.

> *"The greatest leader is not necessarily the one who does the greatest things. He is the one that gets the people to do the greatest things."*
> **-Ronald Reagan**

We know that the greatest leaders are great communicators – think Churchill or Steve Jobs, for example.

Robert Kiyosaki - of [Rich Dad, Poor Dad](#) fame, said: "True communication is the response you get".

And by that, he meant that your communication isn't complete until you see how others react to it.

How you communicate is mirrored in the way people interact with you. So, you need to take ownership of your communication. It is not your team's fault if they misunderstand your messaging - so work on how you deliver your messages to ensure you get the results you want.

What Exactly IS Communication?

Communication is the act of "imparting information" for the purpose of "evoking understanding".

Effective communication is about conveying your messages to other people clearly and unambiguously. It's also about receiving information that others are sending to you with as little distortion as possible.

Communication is not a difficult process to comprehend. It's simply a natural process that takes place when your ideas are transferred to another, and arrive intact, complete and coherent. But mastering this process is a different story.

The Communication Cycle

THE COMMUNICATION CYCLE

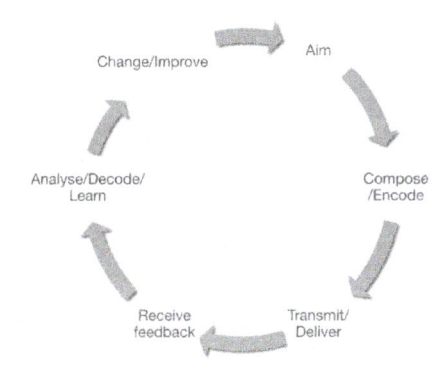

[Diagram: A circular cycle with six steps connected by arrows: Aim → Compose/Encode → Transmit/Deliver → Receive feedback → Analyse/Decode/Learn → Change/Improve → (back to Aim)]

Whether compiling email, delivering training, or giving a presentation, clearly you must communicate clearly, concisely, and coherently.

The Communication Cycle is a six-step process that helps you develop and refine your message. It helps ensure you don't forget anything essential the first time you present it, and it helps you maximise its impact in the times that follow. By putting the process into the form of a cycle, this approach encourages you to use the feedback you receive to improve your communications in the future.

Step 1: Clarify Your Aim

Organise your thoughts about the message that you want to communicate by answering these questions:

- Who am I communicating with?
- What message am I trying to send, and what am I trying to achieve with it?
- Why do I want to send this message? Do I need to send it at all?
- What do I want my audience to feel?
- What does my audience need or desire from this message?
- What do I want my audience to do with this information?

Step 2: Compose/Encode

Now you've organised your thoughts with the questions in Step 1, it's time to start crafting your message.

- Think about:
- What is the best way to communicate this message?
- What level/type of language should I use?
- Does the audience have any background information on my topic?
- Will my audience need any additional resources to understand my message?
- Am I expressing emotions in my message? If so, which emotions?
- Will the audience assume anything about me or my motives that will hurt communication?

Step 3: Transmit/Deliver

How you communicate your message is vital to ensuring your audience receives it effectively. Ask yourself:

- Is this the right time to send this message?
- What is my audience's state of mind likely to be, and what workload will they be experiencing when they receive this message? How should I present my message to take account of this?
- Will there be any distractions that may hurt communication? (Especially important to consider when giving a speech or presentation.)
- Should I include anyone else in the audience?

Step 4: Receive Feedback

This is a key step. Without audience feedback, you'll never know how to improve communication of your message.

- Make sure you include some type of feedback process as part of your communication.
- Do you know how to read body language and use it to steer your presentation?
- If you're giving a speech or presentation, will you allow time for a question-and answer session?
- Will you have a process for getting feedback from your audience?
- When you receive feedback, is it generally what you want and expect?
- Remember to use indirect feedback here too. Did you get the response you wanted from your communication? Is there anything more that you can interpret from the response that you received?

Step 5: Analyse/Decode/Learn

Use the feedback you received in Step 4 to learn and grow. Depending on your situation, you might need to rewrite your message and try again. (One of the benefits of testing your message on a small scale is that you can do this in advance of communicating 'live'.)

- Why did you receive this feedback? What does this tell you about your message?
- What could you have done differently to get the response you wanted?
- Did the audience feel the way you expected them to feel? If not, why not?
- How should you act or behave differently to move forward?

Step 6: Change/Improve

This step completes the cycle. All the feedback in the world won't help you unless you *commit* to learning and changing.

- Respect and respond to the feedback you've received. If you believe it's valid, change your message or behaviour. Identify resources to help you improve (this could include asking colleagues, doing more testing or using surveys, classes, books or seminars).

Skills to Master

There are simply too many communication skills to mention. I believe in the [Pareto 80:20 Principle](#) – that 20% of skills generate 80% impact.

With this in mind, here are some key communication skills to master as you embark on your scale-up leader journey:

Set a communication rhythm

'Routine sets you free'

The faster you are scaling the more communication is needed - even though you seem too busier than ever. It is for this reason you must still have meetings. Don't avoid having them – but make sure your meetings are structured - and be in control of them.

Make them part of your routine.

This frees up both your time and your team's. With consistency, and a disciplined approach to meetings, codifying a simple activity like meetings into a routine will help drive your long-term success

Faster growing companies simply need to ensure a strong structure to meetings. This is a good meeting rhythm for a scale up organisation (see Verne Harnish's book [Scaling Up](#))

LEADERSHIP TEAM IMPLEMENTATION RHYTHM

- ✔ Quarterly Meeting: One Day ➡ **Strategy**
- ✔ Monthly: 4 Hours ➡ **Priorities**
- ✔ Weekly Meeting: 1 Hour ➡ **Big Issues**
- ✔ Daily Huddles: 5-15 Minutes ➡ **Tactics**

Make them fast, punchy, well-structured and with an agenda. Such an approach helps new recruits onboard fast, too.

There are some simple 'golden rules' of organising meetings, which we'd all do well to remember. They are:

- Preparation,
- Time discipline,
- Agreeing the 'rules of the game', and
- Honing meetings skills - such as ensuring good structure, the ability to chair a meeting, and ensuring everyone participates

> *"I think the power of persuasion would be the greatest superpower of all time"*
> **-Jenny Mollen**

Persuasion

A good scale-up leader must be persuasive. And persuasion takes practice.

Your vision cannot be delivered without excellent persuasive skills to drive it forward. Getting your team and clients to buy into your vision means winning them over.

Remember, persuasion invites collaboration between you and your stakeholders. It is not manipulative - rather, it encourages free-thinking. It should motivate and influence your team - through stimulating open dialogue and engagement.

The wisdom of Greek philosopher Aristotle still bears scrutiny today. He identified three factors in effective persuasion — logos, ethos, and pathos.

Logos appeals to the logic, reason, and facts of your argument. *Ethos* refers to your nature — your character, credibility, and authority. *Pathos* involves the emotional state of your team, and is often considered the most important element.

Persuasive communication involves establishing your credibility - based on your position, experience and trustworthiness. Credibility comes through executing your authority, relaying your expertise and developing strong relationships with your team. Build trust by creating an open atmosphere, and listening to your team's suggestions.

Hard evidence is a vital tool in persuasive communication. How many times have you taken on board something after seeing hard facts? Deliver compelling facts with objectivity, consistency and clarity, and you'll win people over.

Seek common ground with your team, a place where you can deliver your needs and interests, while they feel safe delivering feedback and solutions.

Persuasive leaders also hold an emotional connection with their team. Remember, effective scale-up leaders are all about serving others, not themselves - and an emotional connection means gaining trust and loyalty.

Provide clarity on your destination and priorities

If you operate without vision, without clarity on where you are going, two things will happen:

- Everyone will come to you asking what to do, or
- Chaos will ensue

Your task as a scale-up leader is to provide clarity of where you are going – your North Star – and to constantly reinforce that, along with what your immediate priorities are to get you there.

LACK OF CLARITY WILL LEAD TO...

The Tragic Tale of the VASA – Know Your End Point

Image by Jorge Láscar on flickr.com

In the early 1600s, when King Gustavus Adolphus of Sweden embarked on a warship building project, he wanted it to be the envy of the world. He allocated a forest of one thousand trees and an unlimited budget to the mega project.

But he didn't have a clear idea of how the greatest warship the world had ever seen - the Vasa - might look.

Over a number of years, he demanded changes in the size, shape and length of the ship, the number of cannons - and the final quirk, some 700 ornate sculptures to be attached to the ship.

After many years of construction, Vasa was ready to be launched from the port of Stockholm.

Given the lack of vision, it's perhaps no surprise to learn that at the first gust of wind, the ship tilted to one side, began to take on water, and sank in front of the gathered crowds. Some 30 crew members lost their lives in the sinking of this clearly unseaworthy craft.

The famous tale of the Vasa is certainly cautionary - and serves to underline the importance of working towards a clearly-communicated end point.

There's another lesson too - in that no-one involved in the project dare question the king, even though shipbuilders knew the vessel was top heavy.

Team work and open communication might have saved the Vasa and the crew that lost their lives.

Ultimately, no-one was punished for the fiasco.

One good thing to come out of the whole disaster is that the Vasa was extremely well preserved in the icy waters offshore Sweden. The ship was excavated in the 1960, and is now one of Stockholm's most popular attractions, as well as providing an incredible insight into life and shipbuilding techniques in early 17th century Sweden.

Be a Storyteller

In 2006, New York Times Magazine journalist Rob Walker and Joshua Glenn set out to determine how powerful storytelling really is.

They purchased two hundred low value items (their average cost was $1.25), taking care to ensure there was nothing special about them. We're talking about plastic bananas, an old wooden mallet - you know, things with no intrinsic value.

They then contacted two hundred authors, inviting them to become part of a 'Significant Object study', by asking if they would write a story about one of the objects.

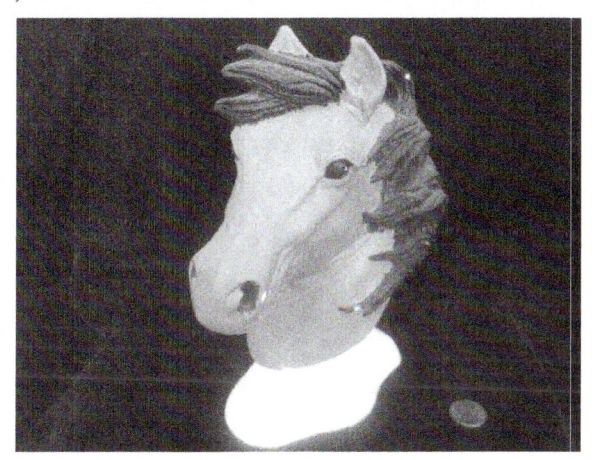

The authors all agreed, and they then auctioned the items on eBay with the stories added to the descriptions. One item, a small plastic horse's head they paid 99 cents for, sold at $62.95 because of the story attached to it.

And the horse's head wasn't a one-off. In total, they spent $197 dollars on the items and ended up selling them for almost $8000. (Profits went to the authors and charities) That's a markup of more than 6300%! And all thanks to powerful narratives.

Stories play on our emotions, and then we become less objective and critically observant. You might say we become more easily duped into buying and doing things we might not do ordinarily.

And the moral of the story is the sheer power of storytelling. Great leaders need to hone great story telling skills, and the greatest leaders employ persuasive storytelling to ensure everyone - staff, stakeholders and customers - buy in to their ideas and vision. As an aspiring scale-up leader, you probably already know a good story helps breathe life into your vision (think Gates, Jobs, Musk). It increases the chances of a message getting through. We are hardwired to engage with stories at a cerebral and heart level - a good story will always elicit an emotional response - and this is why storytelling is a key skill to master!

Communicate clear expectations to your team

> *"Stories are such a powerful driver of emotional value that their effect on any given object's subjective value can actually be measured objectively."*
> **-Joshua Glenn and Rob Walker**

Strangely, this is rarely done. A good leader will ensure the team knows what's expected of them. Communication should be open, two-way, concise and clear. Those reporting to you shouldn't have to guess how you want to work, or how you expect a project or task to play out.

Hopeful trial and error is clearly not conducive to success for your direct reports.

When I worked with Boots, a new CEO, Richard Baker, sent out a memo to his direct reports on the same day he took over, setting out his rules and expectations. By the end of his first day, this had gone through the whole company, providing clarity and setting expectations.

From: Richard Baker   Date: 15 9 03

Re: Richard Baker - "a brief guide"

There a few behaviours that I expect from myself and my teams. I thought it might help you, if I provided an initial insight.

Integrity above all else - integrity is how we behave when no one else is watching. It is saying that what you think honestly and openly, with respect for others. It is killing gossip and seeing the good in others. It is admitting to mistakes fast.... good news can wait.

All of us is better than any of us - teamwork is the secret ingredient. We deliver on promises to each other. We put each other's work ahead of our own. We debate in private, and concur in public. We show trust. We talk each other up in the presence of others.

World-class leadership - we are all leaders in the company. We lead with our ears not our mouths. We say thank you and we look for every opportunity to celebrate success. When success occurs we give credit to others. When failure occurs we take responsibility personally. We start and finish meetings on time and we set a stretching example to others at all times. Development of our people is a priority.

We set the pace - no one in the company will work faster than we do. We must demand the impossible, set stretch goals and be unreasonable to get the job done. Few people know the limit of their abilities. We will make decisions not defer them. We will encourage brevity and simplicity. Complexity is the enemy of pace. Less is more.

Work, rest and play - while working hard, we will also encourage a balanced approach to life. We will take holidays and encourage those around us to do so. We will take our work seriously but not ourselves. Encourage people to have fun. Laughter is the greatest cure of stress and ill-health. Morale improvement is the first step to productivity improvement.

Build Those Bridges

The ability to develop a keen external awareness is what separates great communicators from those who muddle through their interactions with others.

The world's greatest leaders might talk about their ideas, but they do so in a way which also speaks to your emotions and your aspirations.

They realise if their message doesn't take deep root with the audience, then it likely won't be understood, much less championed.

To communicate well, everything we've covered so far should help. Approach communication with an open mind, let go of your biases, expectations and fears.

Learn to actively listen, and take the time to hone your communication skills. Your main concern should be ensuring everyone understands what your goal is, how to get there and why you are doing what you are doing.

Good communication, as with the Boots example above, not only trickles down through the organisation, but builds great bridges with customers, clients and stakeholders.

Exercise: How Good a Communicator Are You?

On each point below, score yourself a 3 or 4 if you are good at that statement, a 1 or 2 if you are not.

- I actively try to retain important facts.
- I repeat the details of the communication to the subject in order to get everything right.
- I avoid getting agitated or hostile when I disagree with the speaker.
- I tune out distractions when listening and I avoid being a distraction myself.
- I make an effort to be interested in what the other person is saying.
- I avoid the use of jargon or industry slang or acronyms.
- I attempt to connect with my audience.
- I adjust my message to my audience.
- I invite questions.

Now add your score up.

Did you score in the **9 to 17** range? You have a LOT of work to do to become an effective communicator.

If you scored **18 to 26** then you do employ some effective communication skills. You may want to identify areas where you can improve and intentionally develop those.

A score of **27 to 35** means you are pretty good to great communicator. You likely work at communicating effectively.

If you got **36**, that's a perfect score and you are truly a great communicator! Someone should take your DNA and clone you.

Coaching Questions:

Who do you admire as a communicator and why?

What methods of communication are you good at? How can you use this method more?

What steps of the communication cycle can you improve upon?

Are there any beliefs holding you back from becoming a better communicator?

CHAPTER 16

Closing Thoughts

> *"Life is about accepting the challenges along the way, choosing to keep moving forward, and savouring the journey."*
> -**Roy T. Bennett**

> *"Only those who dare to fail greatly can ever achieve greatly."*
> -**Robert F. Kennedy**

At this point, it's good to round off your learning experience with a few additional game-changing tools and ways of thinking that will surely accelerate your journey to becoming a scale-up leader.

There's No Silver Bullet

We are bombarded every day with allegedly quick ways to achieve success - get rich, lose weight, find a new partner, become a social media star...

Equally, the internet is awash with ways to create companies, killer products, a million more customers, and easy ways to win business and influence people.

But take a moment to realise that there's no such thing as a 'silver bullet' or 'quick win'.

Nothing is that quick. Everything in life takes application, hard work and skill. It's rare that a 'get rich quick' scheme leads to unlimited wealth in reality. If the 'win' was so easily attained, wouldn't you already be doing it, as would your competitors?

If you've got this far in the book, you already know the journey to becoming a strong, successful scale-up leader is long, tough and not easy for everyone. It takes grit, determination, and a lot of soul searching.

But like every strategy towards becoming a good scale-up leader, I can offer a few final keys to success, which we can all develop. They include focus, discipline and learning.

Focus, Discipline and Learning

Firstly, you need **focus**. You need the insight and concentration to work out what your key priorities are - and the ability to make clear choices. Developing focus isn't easy, but comes with practice, organisation and discipline. Remember, to become focused, you must learn to say no to things - opportunities, new projects, shiny toys - and the more successful you are, the more you'll need to say no to in order to maintain the right level of focus.

Discipline is a key to success. There has to be time and effort involved, week after week, over a sustained period. You are probably acutely aware of the need for discipline in business and in life, if you've got this far. Discipline yourself to focus on your vision, set small, achievable goals on the path, and you'll gradually build in discipline which then leads to long-term gains.

Finally, **Learning** is a tool which just keeps giving. I've stressed throughout the book how we need to read, how we need to be open to new ideas, and how we must learn new skills to remain current and competitive. Success doesn't come simply by taking action, it's about developing the skill to actively learn from what you've done, making adjustments and trying again, over and over.

And what about priorities? Again, sometimes a priority isn't achievable overnight. How about a three-year priority? Ask yourself which 'quick wins' you are focusing on, rather than those activities that will really make a long-term difference to your business or your life?

> *"Look at a day when you are supremely satisfied at the end. It's not a day when you lounge around doing nothing; it's a day you've had everything to do and you've done it."*
> -**Margaret Thatcher**

Focus, discipline and learning are great tools, but of course there's more weapons in the arsenal of the good scale-up leader, which I'm happy to share here.

Think Exponentially, Not Linearly

Jim Collins developed an interesting concept, called the flywheel. We know results don't necessarily happen in a linear way.

He says: "In building a great company or social sector enterprise, there is no single defining action, no grand program, no one killer innovation, no solitary lucky break, no miracle moment. Rather, the process resembles relentlessly pushing a giant, heavy flywheel, turn upon turn, building momentum until a point of breakthrough, and beyond."

He asks us to imagine pushing a giant, heavy iron flywheel. A little push moves it around the axle. Another push, a harder push, and it will turn a little more. You keep pushing, little by little, until one day it spins continuously, thanks to the momentum of your pushes.

From the outside, people simply see a spinning flywheel. They don't know - or understand - that to reach that point has taken considerable sustained effort, focus and discipline.

If someone asked which push made the flywheel turn continuously, you wouldn't be able to answer - the momentum built up with every single push, big or small.

Collins said, in Good to Great, that he kept thinking he'd find "the one big thing," - the miracle moment that defined that special breakthrough.

But the good-to-great executives he interviewed simply could not pinpoint a single key event or moment in time that exemplified the transition.

Changing the goal posts, launching random new programmes and ideas, taking routes that de-focus attention from your goal - these all *stop* the flywheel.

Rather than slowly, organically building your company, if you choose to pursue the 'killer' idea, pursue a fad or a whim, you're only losing sight of the true end goal.

Your results will not be linear. You need to maintain continual efforts to keep your 'flywheel' turning - until you hit that tipping point and go exponential in your growth.

Linear thinking is simply taking one logical step at a time, exemplified in organised, rule-based, logical activities. Society teaches us to think this way.

But exponential thinking means taking bold, huge leaps and bounds.

As Harvard Business Review puts it, "The incremental mindset focuses on making something better, while the exponential mindset makes something different. Incremental is satisfied with 10 percent. Exponential is out for 10X."

> *"The light bulb did not come from the continuous improvement of candles."*
> **-Oren Harari**

Adopting an exponential mindset helps you become comfortable with uncertainty - and more ambitious in your vision.

Straight or curved?

Most of us believe that we put effort into our business, and it grows, and we reap rewards.

We think of it as a linear path. But this simply isn't true.

What happens in business is far more of an exponential curve.

There's a line, with very little results, and then there's growth - often rapid growth.

I know if you take a moment to look at any of the recent business success stories, from Google to Amazon via Tesla, they will have experienced a non-linear exponential growth trajectory.

THINK EXPONENTIALLY NOT LINEARLY

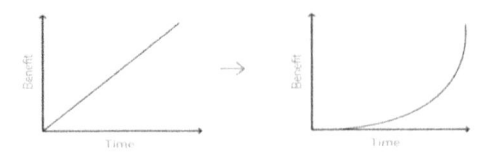

The Size of Your Problems Indicate Your Success

When you're aiming for success, it's a common misconception that there are no problems on the other side of achieving that success.

But for a scale-up leader, success isn't about having surmounted all the challenges - it's about upgrading the quality of challenges you must face.

You have to understand that on the other side of success, there isn't a pot of gold waiting for you, rather bigger, more complex problems. And that should serve to energise you.

I asked one of my clients, a highly successful serial entrepreneur, what he likes to do for fun - and he said in his free time, he enjoys nothing more than dreaming of new problems and writing business plans for new companies!

This is exactly the point - that if you have what it takes to become a successful scale-up leader, you must learn to embrace problems and challenges.

Solving them is what drives you.

So, if you're looking to step up to the plate, stop trying to solve your current challenges and start to focus on how you might take on even bigger ones.

And Always Remember...

Enjoy the journey! The past is the story you tell yourself. The future lives in our imagination. The only time is the present - so always make sure you live the now and enjoy the journey.

Like every aspect of the journey so far, being committed is a choice. An active choice to decide you are fully committed. The speed of growth is entirely in your control. Life is short, so set the right pace for your own journey, and ensure you enjoy the ride.

Coaching Questions

What one goal must you achieve that will have a disproportionate impact on the rest of my life? (Focus)

Who must you BE to deliver this goal?

What habits must you start, stop and continue to allow this to happen? (Discipline)

What skills must you develop to become a Scale up leader? (Learning)

Continuing the Scale-Up Leader journey...

High Growth simply works with the most ambitious and fastest growing companies across the world, providing their leaders with the skills, knowledge, training and tailored coaching needed to achieve sustainable high growth.

We have always aimed to cut through the multitude of tools, strategies and often conflicting information to deliver growth by providing a proven approach, supported by a host of cutting-edge tools. This enables scale-up leaders to deliver growth easily, while enjoying the journey.

How we work with each company is carefully tailored, and based on skills they have, their learning style and pace of ambition. But High Growth's approach is likely to include coaching, workshops and on-going non-executive support.

What Makes High Growth Unique?

Deep Experience

All our directors and accredited High Growth coaches hold a strong track record of business success, having successfully managed their own high growth businesses. We practice what we teach.

A Record of Success

We have an outstanding track record of delivering profitable and tangible results in thousands of companies through our high growth programmes.

A Unique System

Our approach, tools, coaching and high growth training strategies have been developed working with scale-up and high growth organisations, consistently achieving outstanding results.

Cutting-Edge Knowledge

We work with - and learn from - leading business practitioners globally, many of whom are mentors or advisors to High Growth.

Focused

We only work with individuals and companies committed to high growth.

Tailored

No company is the same. Every company learns in its own way, depending on the learning style, makeup of the team and stage of business growth. For this reason, every business High Growth works with receives a bespoke approach.

To learn more about working with High Growth, visit us online at: www.highgrowth.com. Success is at your fingertips. All you have to do is reach out and grab it.

To your success,

Stuart Ross

Stuart Ross

Founder, High Growth

Hungry For More?

Sign up to our newsletter at highgrowth.com

Read our articles here: https://highgrowth.com/read/

Watch some great teaching, coaching and speaking here: https://highgrowth.com/watch/

Subscribe to the High Growth YouTube channel here: https://www.youtube.com/user/HighGrowth1

Follow us on social media:

LinkedIn: https://www.linkedin.com/company/high-growth

Facebook: https://www.facebook.com/highgrowth/

Twitter: https://twitter.com/high_growth

Instagram: https://www.instagram.com/high_growth/

highgrowth

Bibliography

ActionCOACH. *Identity Iceberg*. https://www.actioncoach.com/blog/identity-iceberg/ (2014).

Alcoholics Anonymous. *The 12 Steps of AA*. https://www.alcoholics-anonymous.org.uk/about-aa/the-12-steps-of-aa

Annette O'Toole. *Seven Signs You May Be Unfuckwithable*. https://www.patreon.com/posts/seven-signs-you-27961949 (2019).

Bill Carmody. *Eradicating Your Limiting Beliefs*. https://www.inc.com/bill-carmody/eradicating-your-limiting-beliefs.html (2015).

Brenda Hector. *What The Identity Iceberg Is and How It Helps You Build an Identity*. https://brendahector.actioncoach.co.uk/2021/01/19/identity-iceberg/

Carol Dweck. *Mindset: Changing the way you think to fulfil your Potential*. https://www.amazon.co.uk/Mindset-Updated-ChangingFulfilPotential/dp/147213995X/ (2017).

Charles Duhigg. *The Power of Habit: Why We Do, and How to Change*. https://www.amazon.co.uk/Power-Habit-Why-What-Change/dp/B007ROERCY (2016).

Darren Hardy. *The Compound Effect.* https://www.amazon.co.uk/Compound-Effect-Perseus/dp/159315724X (2012).

Dave Inder Comar. *Your satori moment.* https://daveindercomar.com/blog/2017/12/your-satori-moment

Katie De Jong. *Are you Struggling to Forgive? Try a Little 'Radical Forgiveness'.* https://katiedejong.com/try-a-little-radical-forgiveness/ (2017).

Dr. Paul Brewerton. *Habit stacking - what is habit stacking and how to do it.* https://www.strengthscope.com/habit-stacking-what-is-habit-stacking-and-how-to-do-it/ (2019).

Gary Z McGee, *Seven Signs You May Be Unfuckwithable* (2016).

Hal Elrod. The Miracle Morning: The 6 Habits That Will Transform Your Life Before 8AM. https://www.amazon.co.uk/MiracleMorning-Habits-Transformhighest/dp/1473668948/ (2017).

Heinrich Böll. *Anekdote zur Senkung der Arbeitsmoral.* https://en.wikipedia.org/wiki/Anekdote_zur_Senkung_der_Arbeitsmoral (1963).

Holly Scherer. *Compounding Habits - Small Steps & Massive Results.* https://www.hollyscherer.com/compounding-habits/

Jack Canfield, *Beat the "Shiny Object" Syndrome.* https://www.evolutionaryleaders.net/blog/beat-shiny-object-syndrome/ (2014).

Jack Canfield. *The Success Formula that Puts You in Control of Your Destiny.* https://www.jackcanfield.com/blog/the-formula-that-puts-you-in-control-of-success/

James Clear. *Atomic Habits.* https://www.amazon.co.uk/Atomic-Habits-Proven-BuildBreak/dp/1847941834 (2018).

James Stockdale. https://en.wikipedia.org/wiki/James_Stockdale

Jennie Jerome. In: John Maxwell. *Making an Impression Vs. Being Impressed.* https://www.johnmaxwell.com/blog/making-an-impression-vs-being-impressed/ (2011).

Jim Collins and Morten T Hansen. *Great by Choice: Uncertainty, Chaos and Luck - Why Some People Thrive Despite Them All.* https://www.amazon.co.uk/Great-Choice-Uncertainty-ThriveDespite/dp/B006JPBRDE/ (2011).

Jim Collins. *Stockdale Paradox* https://www.jimcollins.com/concepts/Stockdale-Concept.html

Jim Collins. *The Flywheel Effect.* https://www.jimcollins.com/concepts/the-flywheel.html

Joe Dispenza. *Breaking the Habit of Being Yourself: How to Lose Your Mind and Create a New One.* https://www.amazon.co.uk/Breaking-Habit-Being-Yourself-Create/dp/1848508565 (2012).

Keith Cunningham. *Keys to the Vault.* https://keystothevault.com/

Liz Wiseman and Stephen Covey. *Multipliers.* https://www.amazon.co.uk/Multipliers-Revised-Updated-Leaders-Everyone/dp/B06XY93FWL (2010).

Mark Sanborn. *The Potential Principle.* https://marksanborn.com/product/the-potential-principle/ (2017).

Mike Wyatt. *10 Communication Secrets of Great Leaders.* https://www.forbes.com/sites/mikemyatt/2012/04/04/10-communication-secrets-of-great-leaders (2012).

Norman Maclean. *Young Men and Fire.* https://en.wikipedia.org/wiki/Young_Men_and_Fire (1992).

OECD. *Eurostat-OECD Manual on Business Demography Statistics.* https://www.oecd.org/sdd/business-stats/eurostat-oecdmanualonbusinessdemographystatistics.htm (2007: 82).

Office for National Statistics. *Business demography, UK: 2019.* https://www.ons.gov.uk/businessindustryandtrade/business/activitysizeandlocation/bulletins/businessdemography/2019

Omar Itani. *Always Choose to Focus on What's Within Your Control.* https://www.omaritani.com/blog/learn-to-focus-on-what-is-within-your-control (2020).

Reid Hoffman. https://twitter.com/reidhoffman/status/847142924240379904?lang=en

Rich Litvin. *The opposite of a default future is a created life.* https://richlitvin.com/opposite-of-default-future/ (2021).

Rich Litvin. *The Power of Lazy Leadership.* https://richlitvin.com/lazy-leadership/ (2021).

Richard Rumelt. *Good Strategy/Bad Strategy: The difference and why it matters.* https://www.amazon.co.uk/Good-Strategy-Bad-Difference-Matters/dp/B07R81FHT2/ (2019).

Robert J. Hastings. *The Station: A Reminder to Cherish the Journey.*

Robert T. Kiyosaki. *Rich Dad Poor Dad: What the Rich Teach Their Kids About Money That the Poor and Middle Class Do Not!* https://www.amazon.co.uk/Rich-Dad-Poor-Teach-Middle/dp/1612680194 (2017).

Roland Huntford. *Scott And Amundsen: The Last Place on Earth.* https://www.amazon.co.uk/Scott-Amundsen-Last-Place-Earth/dp/0349113955 (2000).

Roy T. Bennett. *The Light in the Heart: Inspirational Thoughts for Living Your Best Life.* https://www.amazon.co.uk/Light-Heart-Inspirational-Thoughts-Living-ebook/dp/B01CALZ290

Simone de Beauvoir. *Pyrrhus and Cineas.* https://en.wikipedia.org/wiki/Pyrrhus_and_Cineas (1944).

Tony Robbins. *How to Surround Yourself with Good People.* https://www.tonyrobbins.com/stories/business-mastery/surround-yourself-with-quality-people/

Tony Robbins. *The Dickens Pattern.* https://www.youtube.com/watch?v=8awWbuFQL2Q

Tony Schwartz and Catherine McCarthy. *Manage Your Energy, Not Your Time.* https://hbr.org/2007/10/manage-your-energy-not-your-time

Tony Schwartz. *Turning 60: The Twelve Most Important Lessons I've Learned So Far.* https://hbr.org/2012/05/turning-60-the-twelve-most.html (2012).

Vishen Lakhiani. *The Code of the Extraordinary Mind: 10 Unconventional Laws to Redefine Your Life and Succeed on Your Own Terms.* https://www.amazon.co.uk/Code-Extraordinary-MindUnconventionalRedefine/dp/0593135822/ (2019).

Index

A

Abraham Lincoln, 30, 36
Alcoholics Anonymous, 72
Amazon, 198
Amy Poehler, 85
Andy Grove, 22
Andy Murray, 87
Annette O'Toole, 165
Anthony Volodkin, 63
Apple, 22, 87, 102-103, 110
Aristotle, 184

B

Benjamin Disraeli, 141-142,
Bill Carmody, 26
Bill Gates, 135, 154, 187
Bob Parsons, 140
Boots, 188, 190
Brenda Hector, 24
Brendon Burchard, 90
Brian Tracy, 81, 176

C

Carol Dweck, 118, 121
Carl Jung, 172
Catherine McCarthy, 78

Charles Darwin, 99
Charles Duhigg, 63, 70, 72
Christian N. Bovee, 150
Clive Woodward, 125, 140

D

Dale Carnegie, 118
Darren Hardy, 87
Darwin Smith, 136
Dave Inder Comar, 45
David McClelland, 87
Deepak Chopra, 50
Donald Knuth, 152

E

Elon Musk, 44, 108, 110, 135, 163, 187
E. M. Forster, 97

G

Gary Vaynerchuk, 131
Gary Z McGee, 165
George Bernard Shaw, 176
George Eliot, 30
Gloria Steinem, 11
Google, 198
Gustavus Adolphus, 185-186

H

Harvard Business Review, 78, 197
Harvard University, 87
Hal Elrod, 74-75
Heinrich Böll, 37
Henry Ford, 64, 85, 110

I

Intel, 22

J

Jack Canfield, 102, 166
Jack Welch, 106, 110
James Clear, 71
James Dyson, 113
James Madison, 133
James Stockdale, 112-113
Jeff Bezos, 27, 163
Jennie Jerome, 141
Jenny Mollen, 183
Jim Carrey, 114
Jim Collins, 53-56, 85-86, 92-93, 112, 131-136, 196
Jim Rohn, 87
Joe Dispenza, 64-65
Johann Wolfgang von Goethe, 7
John Adams, 133
John Quincy Adams, 140
Jonathan Swift, 106
Joshua Glenn, 186, 188

K

Karl Frei, 171
Katie Goodman, 168
Keith Cunningham, 107, 154-155
Ken Blanchard, 41
Kimberly-Clark, 136
Koshin Ogui, 169

L

Larry Ellison, 162
LinkedIn, 11
Lisa Nichols, 90
Lynda Barry, 21

M

Mahatma Gandhi, 118
Margaret Thatcher, 196
Mark Pincus, 11
Mark Sanborn, 127
Mark Twain, 81
Mary Ann Evans, 30
Mercedes Benz, 52
Michael John Bobak, 7
Michelle Obama, 50
Microsoft, 121-122, 128
Mo Farah, 87
Morten T. Hansen, 53-55

N

New York Times Magazine, 186
Nike, 162
Norman Maclean, 97-98

O

Ogilvy Group UK, 153
Omar Hamoui, 41
Omar Itani, 168
Oren Harari, 197
Organisation for Economic Co-operation and Development (OECD), 2, 11

P

Paul J. Meyer, 33-34
Peter Drucker, 29
Phil Knight, 162
Philippe Petit, 41-43

R

Reid Hoffman, 1, 11
Richard Baker, 188
Richard Branson, 163
Richard Delaunay, 106
Richard Rumelt, 102
Rich Litvin, 66, 152
Roald Amundsen, 55-56

Rob Kalin, 1
Rob Walker, 186, 188
Robert F. Kennedy, 194
Robert Falcon Scott, 55-56
Robert J. Hastings, 52
Robert T. Kiyosaki, 154, 178
Roland Huntford, 56
Ronald Reagan, 177
Rory Sutherland, 153
Roy T. Bennett, 194
Rumi, 171

S

Satya Nadella, 121-122, 127-128
Scale Up Institute, 12
Seth Godin, 90
Shaquille O'Neal, 118
Space X, 108
Spotify, 126
Stanford University, 121, 152
Steve Jobs, 7, 87, 102-103, 110, 135, 178, 187
Steve Maraboli, 97
Steven Pressfield, 63
Steve Scott, 71
Success Motivation® Institute, 33

T

Tesla, 198
Theodore Roosevelt, 169
Thomas Jefferson, 133
Thomas Szasz, 150
Tim Cook, 22, 87
Time Magazine, 141
Tony Robbins, 25-26, 86, 90, 163, 173
Tony Schwartz, 78, 150
Trevor Wilson, 136
TWI Inc., 136
Twitter, 128

V

Verne Harnish, 182
Vicent Van Gogh, 79
Vishen Lakhiani, 90, 162

W

Warren Buffet, 101, 154
William Ewart Gladstone, 141-142
William James, 131
Winnie the Pooh, 130
Winston Churchill, 141, 178

Printed in Great Britain
by Amazon